Preparing for the
Lord's Supper

Preparing for the Lord's Supper

William Bradshaw
and
Arthur Hildersham

Edited and Introduced by
Lesley A. Rowe

Reformation Heritage Books
Grand Rapids, Michigan

Soli Deo Gloria Publications
An imprint of Reformation Heritage Books
2965 Leonard St., NE
Grand Rapids, MI 49525
616-977-0889
orders@heritagebooks.org
www.heritagebooks.org

Printed in the United States of America
19 20 21 22 23 24/10 9 8 7 6 5 4 3 2 1

ISBN: 978-1-60178-660-9 (hardcover)
ISBN: 978-1-60178-661-6 (e-pub)

For additional Reformed literature, request a free book list from Reformation Heritage Books at the above regular or e-mail address.

CONTENTS

PART 2

Showing How to Prevent the Dangerous Sin of Profaning This Sacrament

PART 3

A Brief Form of Examination

The Doctrine of Communicating Worthily in the Lord's Supper
by Arthur Hildersham

INTRODUCTION

A Biographical Summary of the Two Authors

Arthur Hildersham was born on October 6, 1563, at Stetchworth, Cambridgeshire.[1] His family was devoutly Roman Catholic and, on his mother's side, was related to royalty. Hildersham was converted to the evangelical faith during his school days, and he mixed in Puritan circles when he attended Cambridge University. When he refused to comply with his father's demand that he enter the Roman Catholic priesthood, however, his parents disowned him. In his time of need, he was rescued by his relative Henry Hastings, the third Earl of Huntingdon (known as the "Puritan Earl"), who became his patron. After the completion of Hildersham's studies, the earl invited him to become his chaplain and lecturer at Ashby-de-la-Zouch, Leicestershire, in 1587.

Hildersham served as lecturer for six years before he was appointed vicar of the town in 1593. He was a faithful gospel minister, preaching a powerful gospel message. People flocked to hear him, and there were many conversions. However, he

---

1. For more details on Hildersham's life, see Lesley A. Rowe, *The Life and Times of Arthur Hildersham: Prince among Puritans* (Grand Rapids: Reformation Heritage Books, 2013). Some of the material for this introduction is drawn directly from chapter 12 of that book. For Bradshaw's life, see Thomas Gataker, "The Life and Death of Master William Bradshaw," in Samuel Clarke, *A General Martyrologie* (London, 1677), 25–60.

was a ceremonial nonconformist, and this brought him into conflict with the Church of England authorities. He was one of the main organizers of the Puritan Millenary Petition, presented to King James I on his accession to the English throne in 1603. In 1605, Hildersham's nonconformity resulted in his being dismissed from his post as vicar of Ashby, although he was able to continue preaching for some time as lecturer and in the surrounding areas. In 1613 he was banned from preaching completely, and in 1615 he was expelled from the ministry, excommunicated, heavily fined, and spent some months in prison. The unsubstantiated charge brought against him was that he was a ringleader of the "schismatics," stirring up discontent with the established church. Despite this silencing and persecution, Hildersham continued to live among the people of Ashby and served them as a loving friend and neighbor. In 1625, upon the death of King James I, Hildersham was relicensed as a minister and was able to preach again in Ashby in his capacity as lecturer. In the seven years before his death in 1632, at age sixty-eight, he delivered two sermon series. One was on Psalm 35:13 (8 lectures) and the other on Psalm 51:1–7 (152 lectures). He died on Sunday, March 4, 1632, and was buried two days later with scenes of great mourning in the chancel of St. Helen's church, Ashby, where a monument to him was erected by his son Samuel.

Hildersham and his wife, Ann, had eight children, five of whom survived into adulthood. Their eldest son, Samuel, also entered the Church of England ministry and was later ejected for nonconformity in 1662.

William Bradshaw's life was a difficult and unsettled one despite his godly character and gift for inspiring affection. He could count Puritan ministers such as Hildersham, Thomas Gataker, Thomas Cartwright, Joseph Hall, and Laurence Chaderton among his closest friends. He was born in 1570 in the Leicestershire market town of Market Bosworth. His family was poor, but he was offered a free place in Ashby School, from where he proceeded, in 1589, to Emmanuel College, Cambridge, whence he obtained his MA. It was Hildersham who recommended him to the patronage of Sir Edward and Sir Francis Hastings, brothers of the third Earl of Huntingdon, who contributed to his support during his university studies.

While waiting to commence a fellowship at the newly formed Sidney Sussex College, Cambridge, Bradshaw served as tutor to the children of the governor of Guernsey, Sir Thomas Leighton. It was said that when Bradshaw departed from Guernsey he left a "sweet scent" behind him among the family, the French ministers, and soldiers in the island's garrison.

During his time at Sidney Sussex College, Bradshaw entered the ministry and began to preach and lecture locally. In the 1590s he became a target of the hostile church authorities for receiving and distributing prohibited books written by the Puritan exorcist John Darrell, whom Bradshaw had known in Leicestershire. He was forced to withdraw from the university, and from then on he was always a marked man as far as the anti-Puritan bishops were concerned, which made it difficult for him to get ministerial employment.

However, in 1601 a preaching position became vacant in the naval town of Chatham in Kent, to which Chaderton recommended him. Bradshaw's ministry was well received at first, but the following year troublemakers made accusations about him to the bishop of Rochester. Despite the inhabitants of Chatham petitioning on his behalf, Bradshaw was compelled to leave his post when he refused the subscription tendered to him in May 1602. At this low point of his life he returned to Leicestershire where, "by the good hand of God," Arthur Hildersham commended him to his own "bosom friend,"

Master Alexander Rediche, a godly gentleman then residing at Newhall, near Burton-upon-Trent.

Bradshaw found a haven in the home of Alexander and Katharine Rediche for nearly twelve years, where he served as household chaplain. Although they were financially stretched themselves, the Rediches built a little house nearby for Bradshaw and provided him with a modest stipend so that he was able to marry a widow with whom he had become acquainted in Chatham. They had four children. Bradshaw preached regularly at the local church of Stapenhill and was also engaged with Hildersham and others in the preaching exercises at Burton-upon-Trent and Ashby. When persuaded by his fellow ministers to take the chair at meetings, he gained a reputation as the "weighing divine" because of his gift in handling differences of opinion. His preaching, too, was marked by an ability to "pierce deep into the hearts of his hearers."

In addition to his devotional writings, Bradshaw published controversial works on justification, Puritanism, episcopacy, separatism, and baptism. He died in London in 1618 at age forty-eight.

A Print History

In 1609 a little volume appeared in print containing two short treatises dealing with how to prepare worthily to receive the Lord's Supper. The first of these treatises, originally titled *A Direction for the Weaker Sort of Christians, Shewing in What Manner They Ought to Fit and Prepare Themselves to the Worthy Receiving of the Sacrament of the Body and Blood of Christ*, and later renamed *A Preparation to the Receiving of the Sacrament of Christ's Body and Blood*, was by William Bradshaw. Appended to Bradshaw's work, and introduced by him, was an anonymous writing on the same subject, in the form of a catechism, titled *The Doctrine of Communicating Worthily in the Lord's Supper*. This declared that it was intended "for the more familiar instruction of the simple," and it was soon revealed to have been written by Arthur Hildersham, Bradshaw's friend and mentor.

The little volume rapidly became popular: two editions appeared in the first year, and a total of eleven editions were published between 1609 and 1643. It was one of the earliest examples of the specialist "pre-communion handbooks," a genre that reached its peak between 1660 and 1700. In fact, the Bradshaw/Hildersham book was in the top four early modern best-selling titles on the subject.[2] It was small and relatively cheap at ninepence, which, along with its clear and easily understood style, made it readily accessible to a wide market. As both writers explained, they were aiming to reach the simple, the ignorant, and the weak rather than the more educated and affluent elite.

John Cotton, Hildersham's "dear and familiar friend," was among the admirers of Hildersham's treatise. He wrote, "Witness those Questions and Answers, wherein he hath comprized the doctrine of the Lord's Supper...yet have they been of singular good use to many poor souls, for their worthy preparation to that Ordinance. And in very deed they do more fully furnish a Christian to that whole spiritual Duty, than any other, in any language (that I know) in so small a compass."[3]

Thomas Foster, a "humble-minded and sincere-hearted" mercer from Shefford, Bedfordshire, attributed his conversion to reading Bradshaw's treatise. He used to say that "that Book, and that part of it more specially wherein are laid down certain *marks and signs of Faith and Repentance*, was as far (as he was able to deem) the only outward Instrument means of his

---

2. See Ian Green, *Print and Protestantism in Early Modern England* (Oxford: Oxford University Press, 2000), appendix 1, 591–672.

3. John Cotton, "To the Godly Reader," in Arthur Hildersham, *Lectures upon the Fourth of John* (London, 1629).

conversion, through the gracious cooperation of God's Spirit working powerfully and efficaciously upon his heart in the reading thereof."[4]

The Context and Content of the Works

Interestingly, neither Bradshaw's nor Hildersham's contribution to this volume originated as sermons, the most common form of Puritan writing now in print. Both are works of "practical divinity" designed for a very specific purpose. Bradshaw's work began as spiritual advice for Grace Darcy, the daughter of his patrons, the Rediches. In dedicating the work to Grace, Bradshaw explains that his writing originated as "notes lately written forth for your private use." As a gentlewoman with godly parents, Grace was well educated and instructed in the Christian faith, but Bradshaw writes in a plain and fervent style. Obviously he anticipated that other friends would request copies, which is why he was persuaded to go into print.

Hildersham's treatise, which takes the form of a catechism with one hundred questions and answers, was "written some years since by a godly and faithful pastor, for the direction of his own people, in the worthy receiving of the sacrament of the Lord's Supper, at what time he was first called unto them."[5] Hildersham became vicar of Ashby in 1593, sixteen years before publishing his catechism, and it seems that he would have used these questions and answers with his own parishioners in Ashby prior to administering Communion there for the first time. This was a practice recommended by Hildersham's mentor Richard Greenham of Dry Drayton and advocated by Hildersham himself within the treatise.

---

4. Gataker, "Life and Death of Master William Bradshaw," 53.

5. William Bradshaw, "To the Reader," in Arthur Hildersham, *The Doctrine of Communicating Worthily in the Lord's Supper* (London, 1609 and subsequent editions).

Indeed, an earlier manuscript version of Hildersham's work on the Lord's Supper, dating from the 1580s, is still preserved with the Greenham papers in the John Rylands University Library in Manchester.[6] This is very similar to the printed version of 1609, but the original ninety-four questions have been expanded to one hundred, revised and rearranged for a different pastoral situation. The main emphasis in the 1580s appears to have been to persuade readers that the sacrament was still important, whereas by 1609, Hildersham seems more concerned that those who received the Lord's Supper did so in a worthy manner.

The different genesis and purpose of the two works is reflected in their content and style, but a harmony of subject and approach is evident. Bradshaw, writing for an individual as her spiritual counselor, is direct, vivid, and personal. He engages the heart with imagery that sometimes appears almost shocking to modern sensibilities. A key concept for him is the mystery of the sacrament. Hildersham, by way of contrast, writes as a serving parish minister, responsible for the care of souls and for handling contentious issues that so often arose in connection with the administration of the sacraments. He is aware that his congregation includes many simple folk includ-ing tradespeople, agricultural laborers, and servants. He knows that many are ignorant and superstitious; indeed, there are many who are not true believers but who would still expect to receive Communion. He devotes some length to discussing the need for charity between neighbors and how this should be achieved before coming to the Lord's Table—something that does not feature in Bradshaw's work. Hildersham also lays more stress on the role of the minister in examining people before they approached Communion, because this was a way

---

6. John Rylands University Library, Eng., MS 524, fos. 103–11.

of ensuring that his parishioners understood what they were about to do. Church of England ministers were only allowed to exclude notorious offenders from the Communion table, so it was vital that the people were properly instructed beforehand. Hildersham also deals with the matter of private Communions because this was another thorny issue at the time. He includes a section on the appropriate outward conduct to be observed while communicating, something not dealt with by Bradshaw. Hildersham's emphasis is on the six graces a person should endeavor to find in himself prior to communicating: desire, knowledge, faith, repentance, newness of life, and charity. Bradshaw has three prerequisites: faith, repentance, and new obedience. But both men share the concern that a person should approach the Lord's Table with an unfeigned heart, in true faith. Hypocrisy, ignorance, and formalism are all dangers to be avoided.

Bradshaw's treatise is based on one passage, 1 Corinthians 11:23–30, and is followed by a very brief list of questions and answers. Hildersham's work consists entirely of questions and answers, though some answers are very long, constituting mini-treatises in themselves. His catechism does not expound a specific text but is supported by a wide array of biblical proofs.

Because these two treatises have a practical focus, they should not be considered primarily as works of Eucharistic theology. However, it is evident that both authors have a high view of the Lord's Supper and its meaning. Like their Puritan fellows, they were men of the Word and the sacraments. It is obvious, too, that Bradshaw and Hildersham espoused a "Reformed" doctrine of the Eucharist, which was then the prevailing view.[7] They demonstrate quite clearly that they do

---

7. See Keith A. Mathison, *Given for You: Reclaiming Calvin's Doctrine of the Lord's Supper* (Phillipsburg, N.J.: P&R, 2002), part 1, for a helpful historical

not hold the so-called Zwinglian memorialist position; the sacrament "is not ordained to be a bare and naked sign," Hildersham states. Nor, he continues, is it "a picture that puts us in mind of one that is absent, but to be a seal also, with and by which the Lord does verily convey and bestow Christ upon us."[8] Bradshaw talks of spiritually "eat[ing] the flesh of Christ, and drink[ing] his blood…with a believing heart and mind." This emphasis is not surprising considering the influence of Continental Reformers such as Martin Bucer and Peter Martyr Vermigli on the development of the English Prayer Book. However, Bradshaw and Hildersham strongly challenge the Roman Catholic teaching of transubstantiation and the superstitious practices that had left many simple people ignorant and confused.

These treatises are a practical demonstration of what was being taught to common people in ordinary, obscure towns and villages as they prepared to take the Lord's Supper. Similarly, they are a challenge to us today to prepare ourselves thoughtfully and prayerfully before coming to the Lord's Table. In the widest sense, they supply a helpful guide to the proving of our faith by self-examination. As Bradshaw says, "The duty of trying and examining a man's self is of use to the best of Christians."

A Note on the Text and Its Editing
This publication is based on the text of the 1617 edition. Hildersham's work remains essentially unchanged from the 1609 edition, but Bradshaw revised his own work in 1614. He clearly felt that it needed remodeling, something he explains

survey of this subject. I am grateful to Pastor Peter L. Mackenzie for the opportunity to discuss eucharistic theology and for the supply of relevant reading material.

8. Hildersham, *Doctrine of Communicating Worthily*, Question 39.

in a "Letter to the Reader" (included herein). Surprised by the book's popularity, he wished to polish what he considered a rather rough first draft. To be fair to Bradshaw's mature reflection, his revised edition of the text is preferred. After all, Hildersham had over twenty years of honing his own work in manuscript form, taking in feedback and the benefit of practical experience, before he went public in print. Although Bradshaw has reorganized his material, and some sections have been expanded or cut, the core of his work remains the same. A Ramist tree (branched diagram illustrating the method used) that appeared at the beginning of Part 2 of Bradshaw's work in the 1617 edition has been omitted. I have footnoted any other significant changes between editions.

I have endeavored to remain faithful to the original texts so that Bradshaw's and Hildersham's own voices will still speak to us. I have modernized the spelling and altered punctuation to conform to more modern sensibilities. I have provided historical explanations and modern equivalents of archaic words where applicable.

—Lesley A. Rowe

A Preparation to the Receiving of the Sacrament of Christ's Body and Blood

Directing Weak Christians How They
May Worthily Receive the Same

by William Bradshaw

With a Profitable Treatise of the Same Argument,
Written by Another [Arthur Hildersham]

The fifth edition corrected and enlarged

LONDON
Printed by John Beale 1617

To The Virtuous and Worthy Lady, Grace Darcy,[1]

Madam,

Those notes that were lately writ forth for your private use I am now emboldened to make more common, not for any conceited worth in them but to avoid the trouble of yielding satisfaction to other good friends that desire and expect the like office from me. I am sure herein I shall hurt none except myself, nor so much as offend any excepting those for whose use I never intended the publishing thereof.

Your Ladyship's favorable acceptance of them in private has made them thus bold to come forth in public and to grace themselves with the profession of your favor, which is their greatest ornament.[2]

I hope that you, which have given them some entertainment in your closet,[3] will not pass by them as unknown now [that] they present themselves unto you in the street, and the rather for that they come not alone but accompanied and assisted with a most profitable treatise of the same argument, written long since by one whom Your Ladyship reverences

---

1. Grace Darcy was the elder daughter of Bradshaw's godly patrons, Alexander and Katharine Rediche of Newhall, Staffordshire. Grace Rediche married a knight from Kent, Sir Robert Darcy, renowned for his piety and extensive library of theological works. Darcy was one of the close circle around Prince Henry, eldest son of King James I. This work began as private notes for Grace's use, compiled by Bradshaw in his role as household chaplain.

2. The play on Grace's name here is part of an effusive rhetorical style commonly used in such dedicatory epistles.

3. *Closet*: private.

and whose persons and labors in the work of Christ Jesus are (and that deservedly[4]) much esteemed of the people of God.[5] I shall not need to admonish you of the use of either of these treatises; themselves, how little soever, are in that point able to speak for themselves. Only take heed, good Madam, lest in their withdrawing of you from the damnable sin of profaning this holy sacrament you be not by misconstruction brought unto the wicked and superstitious adoration thereof.

Thus in haste, unfeignedly praying the Lord more and more to bless the worthy knight your husband, and yourself, and from heaven to reward those many favors received from you both, I humbly take leave. January 2, 1609.

Your Ladyship's much bounden,

W[illiam]. B[radshaw].

---

4. This phrase has been added since the 1609 edition.

5. Bradshaw is referring to Hildersham's treatise on the Lord's Supper, annexed to his own work.

To the Reader[1]

Let it not offend you, good reader, that in this edition I have varied somewhat from the former. When I first published this treatise, I little thought it should have been thus often called to the press,[2] which (as I suppose) is not so much for any special worth in it as for the worthiness of the other treatise of the same argument, unto which it is adjoined, and which this was a means to bring into the light.

However, seeing by this means it comes to pass that this of mine falls into the hands of many that otherwise (I assure myself) would never have looked after it, and those such as (if it had the author's sense) it would blush to look in the face, being so meanly set out and furnished as it is, I have deemed it fitting this once to review the same and to send it forth in this form you see, wherein some defects in the former are (as I think) supplied, though not so many as either you or I could wish. The old plainness thereof does still continue, which I esteem as no disgrace thereunto, it being by that means fitter for the use of plain and simple-hearted Christians, for whose help and direction I first published it.

Farewell

---

1. This address to the reader does not appear in the 1609 edition. Bradshaw is explaining the changes he has made to his original work in light of its unexpected (to him) popularity. He attributes this to Hildersham's treatise appended to his own.

2. Editions appeared in 1609 (two editions) and in 1615; this was the fifth (two editions appeared in 1617).

PART 1

A Preparation to the Receiving of Christ's Body and Blood

*Showing What a Dangerous Sin It Is to
Receive This Sacrament Unworthily*

CHAPTER 1

Preparation in General, and the Apostles' Form Thereof

No wise man uses to set upon any difficult work, the well performance whereof may be much beneficial and the ill very hurtful and dangerous (such as the receiving of the sacrament of the body and blood of Christ will appear to be), but first (if he can) he sets some time apart to fit and prepare himself thereunto and to forecast that he may do it in the best and most effectual manner. If we go but to an ordinary feast, before we set forth of our doors we use to put on, if we have it, better than our ordinary attire, or at least to brush and make clean and put more handsomely about us that which is upon us.

This sacrament, therefore, being the Lord's Supper, and in that regard more than an ordinary feast, how ought we to dress and prepare ourselves thereunto before we presume to sit down at that table? Surely, if we should bring our souls thereunto in their ordinary habits and attire, we shall do the Master of this feast a great[er] dishonor than we should do to our prince if we presumed to prease[1] to his table in the filthiest habits of chimney sweepers or scavengers.

If, then, we desire to reap fruit and not hurt by this action, if we would have the Lord of this feast to bid us truly welcome

---

1. *Prease*: to hurry on with great speed.

and not to frown upon us, let us before we presume to come thither put on our wedding garments and in that manner fit and prepare our souls (for the feeding of which principally this banquet is prepared), that in the same He may behold a special honor done to Him for preparing such a table and what due account we make of that food which is there set before us.

For the due performance of this work of preparation we cannot follow a better platform than that which the apostle Paul, with his own hand, did draw for a preparation to the church of Corinth in his first epistle, chapter 11:23–33, where for their better preparation to the receiving of this sacrament he teaches them (and us in them) these two points:

1. What a dangerous sin it is to abuse this sacrament (vv. 23–28)
2. By what means the sin aforesaid is to be avoided (vv. 28–33).

If we can be assuredly persuaded of, and soundly affected with, the first and with care and good conscience put in practice that which the apostle propounds in the second, no doubt but we shall then come fitted and prepared to this holy feast and shall with exceeding comfort and delight feed upon that which is prepared therein.

What a dangerous sin it is to abuse this sacrament he shows unto us

1. By propounding the doctrine of the sacrament (vv. 23–27)
2. By inferring therefrom that special sin aforesaid (v. 27).

From which order of the apostle we may learn by the way that ignorance, or want of due consideration, of the doctrine of this sacrament is, and ever has been, one principal cause that so many have abused and profaned the same, and that there is no hope or possibility that those who are grossly ignorant herein should ever with due reverence receive the same and in that regard reap any benefit thereby. But so oft as in this estate they partake thereof, they run their souls upon a dangerous rock. Ignorance may well be the mother of popish devotion, but it is a stepdame to all true Christian piety and the mother and nurse of all superstition, profaneness, and irreligious impieties in God's church.

CHAPTER 2

The Author and Institutor of This Sacrament

The doctrine of this sacrament (as it is propounded by the apostle) is general or special. In the general he teaches us

1. The institutor and the first administer[1] thereof
2. The time when it was first instituted and the religious manner of instituting thereof.

This sacrament was instituted and ordained by Christ Jesus Himself. "I have," says the apostle, "received of the Lord, that which I have delivered unto you" [1 Cor. 11:23],[2] as if he should have said, "If this sacrament had been a device of man's brain, or a human tradition having no other ground but the will and pleasure of man, your abuse and profanation thereof had been the less. But I would have you to consider that this sacrament was ordained and instituted by Christ Jesus Himself and that I delivered this ordinance unto you by express warrant and commission from Him. And therefore, great and damnable must your sin needs be if you shall profane and abuse the same."

---

1. *Administer*: administrator.
2. Throughout the treatise, Bradshaw is using his own translation of the biblical Greek.

They cannot be free from blame who shall contemptuously abuse the ordinances of men, though they require but things indifferent and merely unprofitable; yea, such things as unto the flesh are burdensome and hurtful. Much more blameworthy, then, must they needs be who shall condemn and basely use an immediate[3] ordinance of Christ, who never instituted anything that, being rightly used, is not exceedingly profitable and good—yea, whose very ordaining of it (though before it was unprofitable, or hurtful) makes it good and profitable to the worthy user thereof. It must needs, therefore, argue a base and light estimation of Christ and His wisdom and authority, by rude and irreverent behavior, to abuse any order or constitution of His. And yet what is more ordinary among professed Christians than to make a kind of May game of the principal ordinances of Christ? What palpable contempt is generally offered to the Word read and preached, to prayer, to the sacraments, sabbaths, and the offices of the ministry? How rudely and profanely do many behave themselves in the very solemn worship of God, showing apparent contempt and scorn of the same, as though these ordinances of Christ were but base and ridiculous matters such as are not to be deemed fit for wise men to perform, but in jest and scorn, or (at the best) but as if they were acting and counterfeiting some part upon a stage?

But hence we are to learn that a special means to make us (if we be true and sound-hearted Christians) to see what a foul sin this is, to consider thoroughly and to meditate seriously of this: that in the receiving of this sacrament we do not conform to the humors, conceits, and pleasures of men, of magistrates, or ministers of churches, or fathers, no, nor to the mere ordinances of prophets and apostles, but to the express will and

---

3. *Immediate*: direct.

commandment of Christ. This is in the nature of man, that if they be enjoined or commanded anything by an inferior that has no authority, though the thing required be honest and lawful—yea, good and profitable—yet they will either scorn to do it, or do it in scorn. But if one in authority (whom in that respect they reverence) shall require the same thing, or that which is worse, they will (if they be not very careless and desperate) yield obedience thereunto in fear and reverence.

Except, therefore, we should be so impious as to hold that our Savior has no power to require this duty at our hand, or so shameless and impudent as to defend that He does nowhere require it of us, or so blasphemous as to say He has shown no wisdom therein, we must needs yield that it must needs be a shameful sin to profane this sacrament, which is enjoined to be received by so awful and sovereign authority.

When, therefore, men come so rudely and unprepared to the receiving of these holy rites, as ordinarily they do, it is a sign they never think of that high and sacred authority that has ordained them but only conceit and esteem of them as of certain formalities that custom and long continuance has made a fashion and that men are to conform unto, more to avoid singularity than for any necessity or profit or out of any duty that they owe to the institutor of them.

This, then, is (and ought to be) the main foundation of all true reverence, not only in the use of this but of all other parts of God's worship: *that Christ Jesus requires this service at our hands.* And would the ministers of Christ (who are by their office to dispense these and other the like ordinances of Christ) have their ministry not contemned[4] but truly reverenced, they should make it appear (as Paul does here) that

---

4. *Contemned*: despised.

they minister no other word or sacrament, prescribe no other worship, preach no other doctrine, bind men's consciences with no other laws, allure them with no other promises, fear them with no other threatening than such as they can both say and show that they have received from Christ Himself.

The First Administrator of This Sacrament

Our Savior Christ did not only Himself institute this sacrament but did in His own person, and with His own hand, first of all administer the same: "The Lord Jesus," says the apostle, "the night that He was betrayed, took bread" [1 Cor. 11:23], as though he should say, "If but myself, or any other apostle, or any person inferior to an apostle had instituted this sacrament by commission from Christ, men should (notwithstanding) have feared to lay impure hands upon a thing so holy. Much more when Christ Jesus has not only immediately instituted but was Himself in His own person a minister thereof and the first that did administer the same."

That service and worship required by man's law, framed but by consequence from the Word or according to the general rules thereof, is in a holy and religious manner to be performed. Much more such a service as Christ so immediately and expressly instituted, not trusting to the discourse and wit of man to appoint the same, and that He did so religiously in His own person perform, so that it cannot but argue great impiety in them who shall contemptuously or but carelessly behave themselves in or about the same. Hence we are to learn

1. That albeit this sacrament is administered unto us now by the hands of weak and sinful men, yet they

being the lawful ministers and substitutes of Christ, we are to receive it from their hands as from the hands of Christ Himself, who though He be not bodily yet is spiritually and will be as effectually present now as at the first institution and administration thereof. And therefore, great shall their shame be and fearful their danger who shall presume to put forth profane hands to receive such high mysteries from the holy and pure hands of Christ Himself.

2. It being a great honor to this sacrament that Christ Himself should in His own person administer it, all good Christians should think and esteem it as an honor unto themselves to be admitted thereunto and as a great indignity and disgrace to be excluded therefrom, much more to exclude themselves from the same when they may be admitted thereunto.

3. The ministers of the Word and sacraments also should hence learn to take heed how they presume to administer this sacrament to such persons as they have cause to be persuaded that Christ Himself would deny this sacrament unto, or how they deny it to such as Christ Himself (if He were in their place) would administer it unto. The one is a great indignity to the sacrament itself, the other a more than barbarous wrong to their brethren.

CHAPTER 4

When This Sacrament Was Instituted

The time that Christ, in His special wisdom, made choice of to institute and administer this sacrament was "In the night in which He was betrayed" [1 Cor. 11:23]. This circumstance argues

1. That this special ordinance, which at this time He instituted for His church when He was preparing Himself to the greatest work of love that ever was shown, even to lay down His life for it, must needs proceed from His infinite love and mercy. Gifts bequeathed by friends upon their deathbeds use much to be esteemed, and where they are contemned, there the love of the giver is thought to be despised. If, then, the love of Christ, showed unto us when He was dying—yea, even ready to be put to death for our sake—be dear and precious to us, this sacrament, which at that very time was instituted by Him and as a special legacy bequeathed to His church (for whom He thought not His own precious blood too dear), must needs deserve to be dear and precious to us and therefore a horrible indignity offered by us to abuse and profane the same.

2. This was no time for Christ, who was infinite in wisdom, to spend in instituting needless and

unprofitable ceremonies. The vainest men that are (if not desperately wicked or distempered in their brain) do not use at such a time to abuse themselves about vanities, but their thoughts then use to be taken up with those matters that most necessarily concern themselves and their friends. Far be it then from us that we should think that our blessed Savior should at this time find nothing else to do but to busy Himself in laying upon His church idle and frivolous observances. If men, how miserable soever in their lives past, at such times as this use to bestow the best things they have upon them they most love, we must needs conceive (or exceedingly dishonor our Savior Christ) that this sacrament, which at this time He bequeathed unto all His churches as a special legacy, is of some inestimable price and value and therefore that it must needs be intolerable inhumanity and ingratitude to despise and abuse the same.

3. Our Savior at this time was undergoing the greatest, most painful, and difficult work that ever was or shall be performed, even to offer up Himself a sacrifice for His church, the zeal of which work had now, more than ever, eaten Him up and captivated all the thoughts and affections of His soul so as it was not possible for Him at this time to think of anything else but what might further this work of our redemption and the salvation of our souls. Seeing this, we must needs conclude that this sacrament, being at this time so deliberately both instituted and administered, must needs tend (after a special manner) to the furtherance of our salvation and to make the work of our redemption effectual unto us. To set light by this sacrament is to despise the great work of our redemption and the salvation of our souls, purchased by the blood of Christ.

CHAPTER 5

The Religious Manner of Instituting and Administering This Sacrament

Our Savior Christ, in the instituting and administering of this sacrament, is said by the apostle "to give thanks" and by the Evangelist Matthew "to bless" that which He instituted and administered. By this blessing and thanksgiving, He dedicated and consecrated the outward elements in this sacrament unto that holy and mystical use unto which they are applied. This blessing was an earnest and effectual calling upon God His Father, that He would be pleased to make this sacrament (being duly administered and received) fruitful and effectual to those holy and saving ends and uses for which they were ordained. His thanksgiving was (no doubt) a rendering of special glory and praise unto God for hearing His prayer, and therein for the great fruit and benefit that (through the blessing of God) shall certainly redound unto all those who are worthy receivers of this sacrament.

In that our Savior does in so special a manner bless this sacrament, we may be assured that by this means He has obtained from God a special blessing upon it. For in Him the Father is so well pleased that that may truly and undoubtedly be verified of Him which Balak said of Balaam: "That which he blesseth, is blessed, and that which he curseth, is cursed" [Num. 22:6]. Christ Jesus, therefore, having at His first institution and administration thereof blessed this sacrament (that is, by prayer drawn down from heaven a special blessing upon it), we must not so understand the same as though this blessing touched only that particular supper which then was celebrated at that present. But we are (out of all doubt) to be persuaded that the very same blessing cleaves inseparably to this sacrament (as oft as it shall be administered and received as it ought to be) to the end of the world so that it shall be a blessed sacrament to every worthy receiver thereof. That is, it shall be an instrument of some great and special blessing unto them, and the greater instrument of blessing it is to them, the greater curse it will be to those who shall profane and irreverently abuse the same.

The special thanks that our Savior gives shows that we cannot too thankfully receive this sacrament, and that if we receive it in that manner which we ought to do, that in the same we shall receive that for which we shall have cause to give thanks and praise and glory unto God as long as we breathe. And the more thankworthy [the] gift [that] is presented unto us in this sacrament, the more ungrateful and graceless [are] we that shall carelessly and undutifully receive the same.

CHAPTER 6

Outward Signs and Elements of This Sacrament

Hitherto of that which the apostle teaches in general concerning this sacrament. That which he teaches in special follows:

1. What are the parts of this sacrament
2. What is the end.[1]

For the better understanding of the parts of this sacrament, something is to be premised of a sacrament in general. This word *sacrament* was wont to signify that solemn oath which the Roman soldiers were wont to take, whereby they bound themselves to perform faithful service to the emperor in his wars. Whence the Latin divines have borrowed it, and now by custom it [has] become (in these Western churches) a proper name whereby those outward badges and ensigns of Christianity (viz., baptism and the Lord's Supper) are usually called, because that Christians in the due receiving of them do, after a special manner, bind themselves (as it were by solemn vows and oaths) to do their Lord and Master Jesus Christ faithful service in His wars against the world, the flesh, and the devil.

More especially, sacraments are mystical rites and ceremonies ordained by Christ to shadow and confirm to His church

---

1. *End*: purpose.

the covenant of grace, or mystery of redemption. Mystical rites and ceremonies are certain bodily sensible signs instituted to shadow and represent, in a secret and artificial manner, things spiritual and internal. In every sacrament, therefore, there are two things to be considered:

1. The outward bodily signs
2. The spiritual matter, which is mystically shadowed and set forth by that sign and yet, after a sort, hidden and locked up in the same.

The apostle expresses both [of] these. The signs are

1. Certain outward elements
2. Certain mystical actions in and about the elements.

The elements are bread and wine: "He…took bread" (1 Cor. 11:23); "After the same manner also He took the cup" (v. 25). Wine is not expressed here, but it is implied, and the fruit of the vine is expressly mentioned by our Savior (Matt. 26; Mark 14).

The actions in and about the elements are

1. Breaking and eating of bread
2. Drinking of wine.

These signs considered in themselves are not of such force to stir up any great reverence in the receiving of them, there being no one thing more common in the world than eating of bread and drinking of wine. Yet there is no just cause why, in regard of the commonest of them, this sacrament should be despised, they being matters in themselves both profitable and comfortable. If Christ had not only ordained bread in general for this sacrament but the basest and hardest kind of bread that could be, such as is made of pulse, or bran, or acorns, [and] if instead of wine He had appointed us in this action vinegar mingled with gall to drink, such as He (for our sakes) was content to taste of, it would beseem the daintiest[2] and most queasy stomach (that looks to be saved by Him) to receive the same thankfully, reverently, and religiously. If He had required of us, instead of eating bread and drinking wine, some service as painful (and in itself shameful) as circumcision, it had been our duty to have accounted it (as the Jews did) our honor to perform the same. It is then intolerable insolence to think it a base and contemptible thing upon Christ's special pleasure to eat bread and drink wine at His table to that end for which He has the same.

There are many things that in themselves are of no honor or respect, that in regard of some special use and application are matters of great honor, [such] as the white wand carried before the judge, the cap of maintenance worn before the lord mayor, the sword borne before the king.[3] Though, therefore, these outward signs be in themselves but common matters, yet in respect of that special mystery that is in them, being applied to that use unto which they are in this sacrament (and that by Christ's own ordinance), they must needs be both an honor to Christ and honorable to the due user of them.

In that this eating of bread and drinking of wine here required was at the first institution done *after supper*, as the apostle notes, it shows that this bread and wine, and this eating and drinking, has more than an ordinary use or end—namely, that we are to eat this bread and to drink this wine not so much to satisfy hunger and quench thirst or to nourish our bodies and revive and refresh our vital spirits, for then our Savior would not have administered it immediately after supper, and

---

2. *Daintiest*: most delicate.

3. *White wand, cap of maintenance, sword*: symbols of legal authority.

that a festival supper, when they (who were to receive it at His hands) were filled before with bread and wine. But we must look herein to another more high and special use, unto which it pleases the wisdom and goodness of Christ in this action to advance these common and ordinary things, so that in this bread and wine we must look after bread and wine of another and higher nature, such whereby our souls are to be nourished and refreshed to everlasting life.

CHAPTER 7

Things Signified by the Signs Aforesaid

Hitherto of the outward signs in this sacrament. The mysteries contained in and under these signs, and expressed by them, are the greatest that can be imagined.

The *breaking of the bread* signifies the breaking of Christ's body—that is, all the unspeakable torments that He suffered in His human nature for our sins, which were greater than if His living body had been rent and torn into a thousand pieces and all His bones broken and beaten to powder.

The *eating of this bread and drinking this wine* signifies that special benefit (which the receiver of this sacrament shall reap by the death and sufferings of Christ) if by a lively faith he apply unto himself the merits thereof. "This bread," says our Savior, according to the apostle's relation, "is my body which was broken for you: And this cup is the New Testament, that was shed for many, for the remission of their sins," as it is more plainly related by the Evangelist Matthew. And therefore our Savior bids them *take and eat* the one and *drink* the other, as though He should have said, "This bread, so broken as you see, shall be a sign and token unto you and unto all others that believe in My Name, of that which I have done and suffered in My flesh for you. This wine, more especially, shall be a sign even of that blood, which hanging upon the cross I shed, to purchase the pardon and remission of your sins, which is not such blood as was offered in the Old Testament—namely, the blood of oxen, goats, and sheep—but is in very deed the blood of God and man, whereby the New Testament is sealed and ratified, which offers salvation to all [of] them who shall repent and believe in Me and rely upon the merits of this My bloody passion.

"Therefore, take and eat this mystical bread and drink this wine, and let them be as seals and pledges unto you, and unto all others who shall worthily receive the same. That as verily as with your bodily mouths you eat this bread and drink this wine, and are comforted and refreshed by them, so verily shall your souls taste of, and by the mouth of faith feed upon and be refreshed with, My body and blood. Yea, in and by the eating of this bread and the drinking of this wine (as you ought to do), you shall spiritually eat and drink My body and blood. That is, the merits of My passion shall (by means thereof) be so effectually applied unto you that thereby (as it were by daily food) you shall live everlastingly, so that that which you eat and drink in this sacrament is not only bread and wine but, after a sort, My body and blood, which was sacrificed for you."

Is not, then, this sacrament a mystery to be trembled at? Is it not a brutish sin, without any preparation, to rush upon the same? If we did but eat and drink ordinarily, for bodily necessity or pleasure, it were brutish to run unto the same, as a horse to the trough, not lifting our hearts (at the least) to God in thankfulness for them. How much more brutish it is to eat this bread and drink this wine without due reverence and regard of so high and heavenly a mystery. It were an indignity offered to the great work of our redemption but occasionally to think or speak thereof without reverence. But to be irreverently affected then, when by such a special ordinance it is so effectually represented and applied unto us, must needs be a dreadful and damnable sin.

For the further confirmation whereof, let us consider some special instructions from the particulars in regard of the special analogy between the signs and the things signified:

1. In that our Savior represents His body in this sacrament by bread, He teaches us thereby that His body is to the soul of man as bread is to the body. Bread is the very staff of a man's bodily life, the most general food of poor and rich, that which of all other food can least be spared, that which in hunger men first and principally desire, that the scarcity whereof makes famine, that which if it be plentiful usually makes all other necessaries of this life plentiful, that which we daily feed upon, that which men generally take greatest pains for. Hence our Savior in the Lord's Prayer, teaching [us] to crave all the needful comforts in this life, comprehends all under *daily bread.* And therefore, by like proportion, His body in that manner that is here meant and propounded is the very staff and stay of a Christian life, that without which neither poor nor rich, high nor low, shall live eternally; that which, without all other means, can feed and nourish a man to everlasting life and which of all other means cannot be spared; that which every true Christian soul first and principally hungers after; that [which] the want whereof only famishes and starves the soul; that which they will take the greatest pains and toil to get, and which without the greatest pain and travail cannot be gotten; that which they will desire to feed upon every day and every meal, relishing nothing else without it.

2. In that the bread is broken to signify His body broken for us, it teaches us that it is not simply the

body of Christ by which we are to be fed but His *body broken*—that is, that which Christ did and suffered for us, especially on the cross. For (to speak properly) His body was not broken. It is not, therefore, properly Christ glorified in heaven, or Christ simply God, or God and man that is the bread which a Christian soul, humbled for sin, can digest or relish, but Christ crucified, Christ hanging upon the cross. It is Christ's death that is indeed the life of a Christian. It is Christ and His cross both together that is the bread of life. Yea, not the cross only but the thorns also wherewith He was crowned, the whips wherewith He was scourged, the nails with which He was fastened, the vinegar and gall that He tasted, yea, and Judas who betrayed Him, and Pilate that condemned Him, and the scribes and Pharisees that prosecuted against Him, and all the people that cried, "Crucify him." Christ considered with all these is that spiritual bread that is typed by the material. And without these He cannot be the bread of life to a sinful soul, so that, if there be any transubstantiation in this sacrament, either the bread is turned into all these, or all these into the bread.

3. The use of wine is well known; it does not only (as water) quench the thirst but also exceedingly comfort the heart and refresh the spirits. Seeing then it is the pleasure of our Savior in this sacrament to make wine the type of His blood, it teaches us what effects Christ's blood and the shedding thereof shall have in the souls of all true Christians and worthy communicants. Their spiritual thirst after righteousness and salvation shall be quenched. In the midst of all the horrors and terrors of death and hell, they shall by means thereof be solaced and comforted. This blood, streaming from the sides of Christ, shall

in the midst of their sorrows and griefs and troubles and vexations be as a cup of the most excellent wine to cheer them and revive their spirits and to enflame their zeal. This wine has that efficacy and force in it: that it will turn all the bitter potions (that God's children use to drink) into wine. When the apostles and our Savior were drinking deeply of [the suffering] of the whip, this wine mingled with that bitter potion turned it also into wine. They rejoiced insomuch as they were counted worthy to suffer that which they did, for Christ's sake.

That religion, therefore, which locks from the people the wine in this sacrament[1] does therein also as much, as lies in it, keep from them also that wine which is typed and shadowed thereby, even the precious blood of Jesus Christ, the only wine that can refresh and comfort the soul of an afflicted sinner, which is enough to argue the same to be anti-Christian, if there were nothing else. And the more anti-Christian, the more it maintains that the wine in this sacrament is the very real blood of Christ. What is this but to teach that the true blood of Christ belongs not to them, [and] that if they will be saved they must be saved by some other means, or only by gazing upon and adoring the painted blood of some painted or carved crucifix.

1. This consecrated bread and wine must also (by the precept of our Savior) be eaten and drunk. And thereby we are taught that those only shall live eternally, by the virtue of Christ's body and blood, that feed upon the same, as men's bodies feed upon bread and wine. For as bread and wine, if they only

---

1. Bradshaw is referring to the Roman Catholic practice of denying the wine to the laity.

be looked upon and not taken and received into the stomach, can[not] feed, nourish, or refresh the body of man or preserve life in the same, no more shall the body and blood of Christ comfort and refresh the soul of a sinner, or be a means of spiritual and everlasting life unto him, except they be received and spiritually applied to the soul, as bread and wine are to the body when they are eaten and drunk. Those, therefore, who are the redeemed of Christ must be knit and united to Christ and one with Him, as the bread that nourishes and the wine that refreshes the body is turned into our flesh and made one with it. This sacrament, then, which seals so great a mystery as this is, cannot be profaned without great indignity to the mystery itself.

2. In that Christ says that that which they take and eat, it is His body, and that which they drink, it is His blood, He teaches us that this sacrament does not only (as in a table) picture and represent what Christ has suffered for sinners, but, which is a thousand times more, it is by the ordinance of Christ (to the worthy receiver) a blessed instrument by means whereof Christ Jesus and His merits are applied and made effectual to their souls. Such is the union of the thing signified and the sign that in and through the eating of this bread and drinking this wine the soul of the worthy receiver does spiritually and by faith eat the body and drink the blood of Jesus Christ, and always finds such strength, comfort, and life therein as the body finds ordinarily in the eating of bread and drinking of wine. This bread and this wine are not only naked signs of Christ's body and

blood, as the garland and ivybush[2] are of wine, which only show that there is wine there to be bought but does not exhibit it. But the body of Christ is in such a manner in this sacramental bread, and the blood in this wine, that in the eating of the one the worthy receiver eats the other, and in drinking the one, drinks the other. Can there then a greater mystery be delivered by man in and about which he ought to be reverently conversant and religiously and holily affected? And is it not a brutish sin to behave ourselves unworthily in such an action?

Let us not here pass by, but once again enter into consideration of, that execrable religion of the Church of Rome, which keeps such a cup, filled with such wine (without any color in the world), from the people. They say that the blood of Christ is in the body of Christ, and therefore the people in receiving the one receive therein the other. But this is an anti-Christian foppery; how can those be together that Christ has so directly put asunder—the one in a loaf, the other in a cup? How can the blood be in a body broken and pierced? How can that blood be in the body which is shed out of the body? What blood of Christ can comfort a Christian soul but that which was shed? Or what blood is offered in this sacrament but that which was shed? And though it were in the body, as it is received in this sacrament, yet was it Christ's will that His blood should not only be eaten but drunk? What a sacrilegious lewdness is this, where Christ especially and by name requires the drinking of His blood, that they should deny the people that and make them take up with the eating of it only? And how does it appear that the blood, as it is eaten, is any

---

2. *Ivybush*: a bush or branch of ivy formerly hung at a tavern door, the ivy being sacred to Bacchus, the Roman god of wine.

part of the sacrament? And if not, what benefit comes to the receiver thereby in that regard? Just nothing. It is the drinking and not the eating of Christ's blood in this sacrament that must refresh the soul of the communicant, and without this drinking thereof, the soul can no more be refreshed with the blood of Christ in this sacrament than the bodily thirst can be quenched by that water which is in bread. And a man—in eating the body of Christ broken, crucified, pierced with a spear, and sacrificed, so as it is exhibited to a Christian—can no more be said in and thereby to drink the blood of Christ than the Jews that did eat the flesh of sheep and oxen offered in sacrifice, after that the blood was separated and the parcels were roasted and broiled, could be said then and therein to drink the blood of sheep and oxen. And they might as well prove that wine was in the bread before the consecration as that the blood of Christ is in the body after the consecration.

CHAPTER 8

The End and Use of This Sacrament in Respect of the Communicant

Hitherto of the parts of this sacrament. The main and most general ends[1] and uses follow, which are two:

1. Respecting ourselves especially
2. Others also.

That which respects ourselves is that we receive this sacrament to solemnize thereby a special memorial of Christ and of our redemption by Him. "This do," says our Savior, "in remembrance of me" [1 Cor. 11:24].

One end, then, why this sacrament is to be used, and the use to be continued in the church of Christ, is that in and by the due receiving thereof we might the more feelingly and effectually remember what our Savior has done and suffered for us.

When our special friends upon their departure from us do bestow upon us any token of remembrance, they do it not only for that special good that comes to us by the ordinary use of the thing itself but also that thereby, so often as we look upon the same or use it, we should moreover make this use of it: to call to mind thereby the many loves and favors they have shown unto us. And this is written in our nature, that when

---

1. *Ends*: purposes.

any occasion is but offered unto us of remembering a dear friend departed from us, to be more than ordinarily affected therewith. Hence superstitious persons so heartily (upon any occasion of remembrance) pray the Lord to have mercy on their souls that are departed this life whom they love and have been bound unto. But when they behold any special memorial and token of their love, then they are often (for the time) transported and ravished with extraordinary affection, which they will show even to the token of remembrance itself, doing a kind of honor unto it. Seeing therefore this sacrament—that is not only left unto us by the greatest friend that ever we had but left of purpose to be a special remembrance and pledge of the greatest love that ever was shown to mortal creatures, and which has the very effects and fruits of love written upon it, yea engraved in it, yea in some sort contained in it—is it not incredible that any that love and believe in Jesus Christ should lightly regard and unworthily abuse this sacrament?

But here, by the way, we may observe how strangely forgetful even the faithful are of the unspeakable love of Christ, that they should stand in need of such a remembrance. For unto them is this sacrament given, as a help thereunto. Is it possible that a man should be forgetful of such a Master as has with a great price redeemed him from the galleys?[2] Yea, who for to redeem him has made Himself a slave, yea, who was content to purchase His servants' freedom with His own death? Is it possible such a servant should need any special remembrance? Would not one think he should rather need some means to make him forget His love? Yet this is the strange disposition of all Christians, even of the best, that though our condition was a

---

2. *Galleys*: When Bradshaw was at Chatham, he was horrified to witness the terrible sight of men being forced to work as slave labor in the galley ships.

thousand times more miserable than the condition of a Turk's galley slave can be; though Christ Jesus has done ten thousand times more for our freedom therefrom than is possible for any one man to do for another; though whatsoever we enjoy we have it from His mercy and love—our souls, bodies, senses, wit, beauty, wealth, life, so as all our senses are so compassed about with memorials of His love that we can [neither] see, hear, feel, nor taste anything but it may put us in mind of His love, yea, of His death and passion by which the free use of these things have been purchased unto us—yet for all this you see we stand in need of a more special remembrance. Yea, and yet (sinful wretches that we are) we are ready to abuse these remembrances, and (which exceeds wonder) we are prone, in the midst of them, most of all to forget Christ and His love toward us, and then and therein readiest to dishonor Him. We may hence further note

1. That Christ our Savior takes it most kindly when we remember and think upon Him and that which He has done for us.

2. The institution of this sacrament to this end shows He much affects and desires it. And the more He affects and delights in our remembrance of Him, the more unkindly and offensively He will take our forgetfulness of Him.

3. Hence also it appears when we specially eat the flesh of Christ and drink His blood, when with a believing heart and mind we effectually remember, and in our remembrance we seriously meditate of, and in our meditation are religiously affected, and in our affections thoroughly enflamed with the love of Christ, grounded upon that which Christ has done for us and which is represented and sealed unto us in this sacrament.

CHAPTER 9

The End and Use of This Sacrament in Respect of Others

The end that respects others is *the showing forth of His death till He come.* That is, by eating this bread and drinking this wine, Christians are to testify and profess and, after a sort, to preach to others even unto the world's end the mystery of the gospel—the sum, substance, and accomplishment whereof is in the death of Christ and the fruits that flow therefrom, all which are represented in this sacrament.

Therefore, in our due receiving of this sacrament, we do (as it were) lead men by the hand into the garden of Gethsemane and there show them Christ in extreme horror sweating blood, Judas traitorously kissing Him, the soldiers binding Him and leading Him to judgment. We lead them to Caiaphas's hall and Pilate's throne and there show them Christ most unjustly condemned, most contumeliously[1] buffeted and spat upon, scourged and crowned with thorns, scorned and derided. We lead them to Mount Calvary and there show them Him nailed on the cross, drinking vinegar mingled with gall, pierced with a spear, forsaken of His Father, in the horror thereof crying out most bitterly, "My God, my God, why hast Thou forsaken Me?" [Matt. 27:46]. And all this for our sake, that thereby He

---

1. *Contumeliously*: scornfully, insolently.

might free us from the curse of the law and purchase for us everlasting life.

Can we in this mystery see and behold all this? Shall we (after a sort) hereby point it out unto others, and shall we therewith be nothing affected in our own souls but come unto the receiving thereof as so many senseless blocks? By this it appears how forcible the doctrine of the sacrament is, to terrify all Christians from the profanation thereof and consequently to the fitting and preparing of them to the worthy receiving thereof.

To conclude, note that the apostle in all the former points has propounded nothing unto the church of Corinth but what they could not be ignorant of before, which practice of the apostle teaches us of what necessity continual teaching is in the church of Christ, when ministers must be fain[2] not only to instruct the people of God in those points of doctrine that they are ignorant of but often also call to their mind and consideration those points that they know already well enough, upon such particular occasions as they are to make special use of them. And verily, though men could say all the Scriptures by heart, though they could understand every hard and difficult place thereof, though they knew all the grounds and principles of the Christian faith, though they were able to answer all oppositions against any divine truth, yet for all this there would be use both of reading the Word and preaching also in the church of God.

For let our knowledge be never so great, yet if we be not often put in mind of it, if we be not taught how in such and such particular cases to apply it, if by the power of Christ's ordinance it be not beaten out of our head [and] into our

---

2. *Fain*: wont, compelled, eager.

heart, it will be as a dead letter unto us, yea, and most out of our head when we should most use it. For so was the particular knowledge of this sacrament in this church of Corinth. And so will the knowledge of this or of any truth else be if it be not revived and quickened in us by daily teaching and instruction.

What It Is to Be Guilty of the Body and Blood of Christ

Hitherto of the doctrine of this sacrament. The consequent of the doctrine follows.

"Whosoever therefore," says the apostle, "shall eat this bread, and drink the cup of the Lord unworthily, shall be guilty of the body and blood of Christ" [1 Cor. 11:27].

We have in the consideration of every particular point of doctrine concerning this sacrament inferred generally that it must needs be a fearful sin to profane and abuse the same and not to receive it in that manner that we ought to do. But the apostle herefrom infers in special a monstrous, dangerous sin indeed.

For the better understanding therefore of the apostle's consequent, and for our further help in this preparation, let us consider

1. The sin itself and the means by which we are guilty of the sin

2. The ground upon which such persons are guilty.

The sin is *a guiltiness of the body and blood of Christ.* To be guilty of His body and blood is to offer some special disgrace and indignity unto the person and sufferings of Christ and (in a special manner) to sin against the great work of our redemption—yea, in some sort, to commit a sin of the very same nature and quality that they did who had their hands in crucifying Christ. For to be guilty of blood is in some sense or other to be a murderer and shedder of blood, and therefore to be guilty of Christ's blood is (in some degree or other) to have our hands in His death and by consequent to be partners with Judas in betraying Him; with the wicked Jews in crying, "Crucify him"; with Annas, Caiaphas, and Pilate in condemning Him; with the cruel soldiers in whipping and scourging Him, spitting in His face, crowning Him with thorns, and nailing Him on the cross; and so on. The worst among Christians abhor these persons, even for these sins committed against the person of Christ. Let us therefore learn to abhor that practice which will pull upon our heads the guilt of the same sin. To be guilty of any blood (though of wicked and sinful blood) has been a burden that has made the stoutest heart to ache and groan under it. But who is able (when his conscience shall once be awaked) to bear the guilt of innocent blood? And if the blood of innocent Abel did lie so heavy upon Cain (Gen. 4:13), how heavy shall the blood of the innocent Lamb of God lie upon them that are guilty thereof? We may remember how heavy it was upon Judas (Matt. 27:25), and we may see at this day how heavy it lies upon the whole nation of the Jews, according to their own cursed wish (Matt. 27:25). This sin, therefore, being a bloody sin and by consequent in itself a most unsupportable sin, can we be too careful to avoid it? It is not our ignorance or good meaning that in this case will justify us. Many of the Jews did in their ignorance crucify Christ (Luke 22:34; Acts 3:17). This church of Corinth also (no doubt) had a good meaning in receiving this sacrament. Yet by not receiving it in that manner that they ought, they were deeply guilty of that foul sin.

CHAPTER 11

By What Means in Receiving This Sacrament Men Become Guilty of the Body and Blood of Christ

The means by which we become guilty of the body and blood of Christ aforesaid is *by receiving this sacrament unworthily*. To receive the sacrament unworthily is to come to the Table of the Lord and there presume to eat this bread and drink this wine without any due reverence or respect of the mystery that is contained in them, or of the end why they were ordained, or of the person by whose authority they were ordained, or without taking any care or thought beforehand to be such kind of persons as this sacrament was ordained and appointed for. The best of men cannot be said (in themselves) to be worthy to receive this sacrament. Yet how unworthy soever we are in ourselves, if Christ deem us as worthy and we be (in some measure) such persons as He has ordained this sacrament for, and if we do our uttermost to receive it in that manner, with such hearts and affections as He requires, we may be said (how unworthy soever otherwise we be) to be worthy receivers of this sacrament.

The ordinary and most common causes and means of unworthy receiving are these that follow:

1. The first (that which we noted in the beginning) is *ignorance*, when men will presume to partake these mysteries before they understand or have learned

(in any reasonable sort) the true meaning and use of them. Such must needs receive hand over head,[1] they know not nor care not what. And how, then, can they possibly be worthy receivers of so high and heavenly mysteries?

2. *Want of special faith*, when men partake of the outward elements yet do not believe or expect any such special fruit or benefit from the receiving thereof as is promised by the Word.

3. *Superstition*, when one comes to the sacrament in a fond conceit and imagination that he shall receive other manner of blessings and benefits by it than is revealed in the Word or promised or intended by Christ.

4. *Sensuality*, when men so satiate and pamper themselves with the delight and pleasures of the world and the flesh as they cannot, nor care to, taste of things spiritual. And therefore they bring no other hearts or affections unto this sacrament than unto ordinary meat and drink, and sometimes worse.

5. *Carelessness* and *security*, which is when we come with such affections and dispositions unto this sacrament as to a matter that we neither look to receive any good by nor fear to receive any hurt by, and therefore care not, so we receive it how we receive it.

6. *Presumption*, when we never care in what manner we receive and yet presume to receive as much fruit and benefit by the sacrament as those who are most careful to fit and prepare themselves thereunto.

7. *Uncharitableness*, when our souls are so full of bitter hatred and malice toward our neighbor, and by means thereof so vexed and disquieted with devilish

---

1. *Hand over head*: headlong, thus rashly, thoughtlessly.

perturbations, that they cannot receive or taste the sweet comforts represented and offered in this sacrament.

8. *Temporizing,*[2] which is when the only or main ground for which we come to receive this sacrament is the fashion and custom of the times and places in which we live, and when without any further examination we think we have done enough if we have (in that outward form and manner) received what others do.

9. *Inconsideration,* or an unstayed and wandering mind, when either we consider not what we are about or have our thoughts (during that action) busied about other matters.

10. *Profaneness,* when we bring such hearts to the receiving of the sacraments as (out of that action at least) despise religion and make a scorn of all true practice and profession of piety.

Other means and causes there are of this sin, but the consideration of these may suffice. As therefore we desire to be worthy receivers of this sacrament, and so to have our hands free from the blood of Christ, let us with all care and study practice the contrary virtues.

---

2. Points 8–10 have been added to the 1609 edition.

CHAPTER 12

Why Unworthy Receivers Are Guilty of the Body and Blood of Christ

The ground and reason why those who receive unworthily are guilty of the body and blood of Christ may be gathered from the former doctrine of the sacrament. For from that does the apostle infer and conclude the same.

1. Such persons in so doing do plainly despise the sacred authority of Christ, the institutor and first administer hereof. Now they that despise the authority of Christ do therein (in some sort) despise the person of Christ and His sufferings, and by consequent show contempt unto His body and blood, by which principally His authority is ratified and confirmed. And to despise the person, sufferings, body, and blood of Christ, what is it (but in some sort) to assent unto and therein to join with them that crucified Him and shed His blood?

2. They contemn[1] a special token of His love, a special memorial of His body and blood, a special instrument by means whereof His body and blood is applied unto them. What is this but to offer an indignity unto His sacred body and blood?

---

1. *Contemn*: despise.

3. They offer herein contempt to the principal cognizances[2] and ensigns[3] of Christianity, to a special coin and picture of Christ crucified.

The like wrong offered to the ensigns and picture of a prince is worthily judged to be offered to the prince himself. Yea, forasmuch as in this sacrament the very body and blood of Christ, and all the benefits depending thereupon, are spiritually offered unto the receiver, as lands are offered and conveyed to men by the sealing and delivering of deeds and indentures, he that shall unworthily behave himself in the receiving of this sacrament shall therein as much despise the body and blood of Christ as he may be said to despise the gift of lands that contemns the writings, seals, and indentures whereby they use to be conveyed, secured, and confirmed. Hence from this consequent we may note

1. That Christ receives damnable indignity and contumely[4] sometimes, not from Jews and infidels only but often from Christians, such as look to be saved by His blood-shedding, and that when they are performing special worship and service unto Him. For what greater wrong can there be than to be guilty of that blood which was shed to redeem us? This was the sin of this church [in Corinth] and is the sin of all such persons as are unworthy receivers of this sacrament.

2. The bare conformity unto the outward exercises of religion, whether Word, prayer, or sacraments, is not enough to make us good Christians, but we may be the worse Christians for this (Rom. 2:28; 1 Cor.

---

2. *Cognizance:* that by which one is known, a badge.
3. *Ensign:* a badge or mark.
4. *Contumely:* a scornful insult.

10:1–7). Many ignorant and seduced souls think they are Christians good enough if their foreheads have been sprinkled with the water of baptism, if sometimes they hear the Word, and [if they] receive the outward elements of this sacrament. But they may do all these in such a manner that by doing of them they may crucify Christ and trample His blood under their feet. It were better for us never to receive this sacrament than in and by the very act thereof to pull upon our heads the guilt of Christ's body and blood.

3. Note the different and contrary effect of this sacrament in the receivers thereof. It is the savor of death unto death to some—to other some, the savor of life unto life. The worthy receiver is fed and refreshed and nourished by the body and blood of Christ received therein. Contrarily, the unworthy receiver is polluted and defiled thereby, and the oftener he receives it, the more he receives therein the bane and poison of his own soul. Those, therefore, that in such a manner receive the body and blood of Christ and look for grace thereby are therein as fond[5] as if they that whipped Christ and nailed Him on the cross (and by means thereof had their faces, hands, and garments besprinkled with His blood) should think by that means to be purged and freed from their sins. Or as if he who pierced Christ's side with a spear should have held a cup at the wound and filled it and drunk it off and have fancied by that means to drink the blood of Christ, to the health and eternal salvation of his own soul.

---

5. *Fond*: foolishly hopeful.

And thus much of the first part of preparation, wherein we have been plainly taught by the apostle what a dangerous sin it is to abuse this holy sacrament. God grant that the consideration hereof may deeply affect us, that we may with fear and trembling take heed what hands we lay upon so holy mysteries. Amen.

PART 2

A Preparation to the Receiving of Christ's Body and Blood

*Showing How to Prevent the Dangerous Sin
of Profaning This Sacrament*

CHAPTER 1

The Method of This Second Part

The apostle, by whose line we draw the doctrine of preparation, having set forth the odiousness of that sin whereby the holy sacrament is abused, does afterward in the words following prescribe a special remedy how that sin may be prevented. In the due conscionable[1] practice whereof does our second part of preparation consist.

The means and remedy aforesaid consists in certain special and necessary duties, to be performed by every Christian that will (to his comfort) partake of this sacrament. The duties the apostle propounds are two:

1. That a man try, search, and examine himself before he presume to receive
2. That he give not over trial and examination of himself till he have found that which he seeks for.

In the first duty we are to consider the trial itself—first, generally, [then] second, more specially—and then the persons that are to make this trial.

---

1. *Conscionable:* regulated or governed by conscience.

CHAPTER 2

The Trial of Ourselves in General

The trial and examination of ourselves in general here required is a diligent search and inquisition to be made within our souls and consciences, whether we be such kind of persons as may be assured that the Lord will bid welcome to this Table. And this trial is not to be slight and cursory but most strict and accurate, such as goldsmiths use when not only by touch but by fire and hammer they try whether their gold and silver be pure or no. For such a manner of trial the apostle's words signify.

The Lord cannot bid any welcome to His Table but such as He is actually reconciled unto and whose persons are acceptable and well pleasing unto Him. They who are such persons have certain special gifts and graces bestowed upon them, from which they may conclude infallibly that God does love and favor them, which for distinction's sake from other common gifts are called *saving graces*.

Herein, then, we must labor to search out in ourselves these graces and to try whether they be in us or no. But before we come to particulars, hence we may note in general

1. That God's special saving graces may be in us and yet not always apparent unto us, but may sometimes lie hidden in the soul until by some special search they may be discovered, else such trials as these should

be needless. As therefore it is a matter of humiliation to all good Christians that upon due trial they find more corruptions in themselves than did before appear unto them, so this may be a special comfort that there are also in them (which by diligent trial they shall find) greater graces than ever they imagined to be in themselves. This, therefore, should encourage us to search ourselves so much the more narrowly. For if we shall (by a careful search) find in our souls but any one grace—or but any degree of a grace—more than we did perceive before, it will bring more sound comfort and joy unto our hearts than if we had found a hidden treasure of silver or gold.

2. By this it appears that a man (if so be he will carefully use the means) may come to some certain knowledge and insight of the saving gifts and graces of God that are in his own soul. And therefore it must needs be a great fault in him to be careless in using the means. It is a sign he sets no price upon God's graces that [he] makes no inquiry whether he has them in his possession or no. Men use to make diligent inquiry after hidden and concealed lands and treasures; much more ought we to search out the concealed graces of God that lie hidden in our own souls and that we cannot employ (as we ought) so long as we know not whether they be in us or no.

3. It is in this respect very beneficial and profitable for us to find out and know what gifts God has bestowed upon us, in that (as it appears by this place) it is a means not only to prevent fearful and dangerous sins but to make us more capable of greater graces that otherwise shall be withheld and detained from us. For we have no grounded hope to receive any

new grace or blessing from any ordinance of God until by a diligent search of ourselves we have first found some former grace in ourselves that may make us (in some degree) fit and worthy receivers thereof. For to him that has (says our Savior) shall be given, and from him that has not shall be taken away, even that which he has. The use of one grace is to fit and prepare us for the receiving of another.

Those special gifts and graces that are in all them whose persons are acceptable to God are *faith* and *repentance*.

By *faith* we are to understand a true, saving, and justifying faith, which is a supernatural gift of God whereby a man (seeing the vileness of his sin) relies only upon the merits of Christ Jesus for the pardon thereof.

From this faith do all other Christian graces proceed, and according to the growth of it do they grow. Whatsoever is done by virtue of this faith (how simple soever the action may seem to be) it is pleasing to God; otherwise, how glorious soever, it is odious to Him. This grace entitles us to Christ and all His merits. This effectually applies them unto us. This is the only mouth by which the body and blood of the Lord is eaten and drunk, and therefore [it is] a special argument of God's favor and a necessary quality to be in all worthy communicants. And therefore we are to make special search and trial of it.

CHAPTER 3

The Trial of Our Faith by the Grounds Thereof

We may try our faith first by the ground, then by the subject. The ground of true saving faith is the Word of God manifested unto our consciences by the Spirit of God to be the Word of God. That faith which rests upon any other groundwork or foundation can be no true saving faith.

A good means to try whether our faith be indeed grounded upon the Word of God is to examine our consciences in these particulars:

1. Whether we believe indeed and in truth that the writings of the prophets and the apostles in the Old and New Testaments are the very Word of God (for the whole Word of God, so far as is needful to be believed unto salvation, is contained therein), or at the least whether we be exceedingly troubled and grieved in our souls, and from our very hearts, when (through any temptation) we are moved to doubt of the same and whether we use all means we can to come to be fully persuaded of [it]. For in such cases God accepts the will and endeavor for the deed.[1]

---

1. Mark 9:24; Rom. 7:18; Matt. 5:6.

2. Whether we unfeignedly desire to be taught and instructed in the Word of God and to come to the true knowledge and understanding and belief thereof, and whether we love and affect those means most that are most powerful and effectual to that end and purpose. For he whose faith is grounded upon God's Word has his hope grounded upon the same Word, even all the hope that he has of everlasting life. And therefore he must needs desire to be acquainted therewith by all means possible.

3. Whether our ignorance and dullness in understanding of the Word, and our forgetfulness thereof, be grievous and troublesome unto us. For how can it choose but grieve and trouble a man when he knows not, or understands not, or cannot remember the evidence of his own everlasting estate?

4. Whether our reading or hearing the Word read or preached, [and] our meditating, conference, and study of it, do increase or nourish our love and delight and belief in it.[2] Or, if we cannot discern any such matter, whether we be not unfeignedly grieved and humbled for it.

5. Whether we give credit and authority unto it above all human traditions and customs whatsoever, and whether we do not deny credit and belief unto whatsoever we know to be repugnant unto the same Word.[3]

6. Whether we find a lightness and cheerfulness in our consciences when we have done anything agreeable unto the Word of God, and whether we find a trouble

---

2. Ps. 119:92, 97, 98, 103.
3. Ps. 119:113.

or dullness and heaviness in the same when we have done anything that we know to be repugnant unto the same Word.

7. Whether we unfeignedly hope in the promises, fear the threatening, desire the blessings, and endeavor to avoid the curses contained in this Word, and whether we equally believe the one as well as the other.

8. Whether we judge it a singular blessing of the Lord that He has in this manner revealed His will in the written Word and that He vouchsafes us liberty and means to come to the knowledge, understanding, and belief of it, and whether we judge it to be a great judgment and curse upon them from whom this Word is hid and who want this liberty and means that we enjoy.

9. Lastly, whether we can prove those points of religion and faith that we hold and believe by the written Word of God, whether we do therefore believe them because we know that they are affirmed in the Word of God, and whether we misdoubt and suspect all those points of religion that we cannot see warranted by the Word of God.

If we can find these properties in our souls, then we have found in ourselves so many infallible signs and tokens that our faith has a true and sound ground.

CHAPTER 4

The Trial of Our Faith by the Object or Matter Thereof

Secondly, we are to try and examine our faith in Christ, whether it be true and lively, no or yea, by the object and matter thereof. The object and matter of true faith is that divine truth which God in His Word has revealed unto us. For if the testimony of God in His Word be the ground of our faith, then that truth (which is revealed in the Word) must needs be the object and matter thereof. Now forasmuch as there was never any one man that could ever attain unto the knowledge of all and every particular truth revealed in the Word of God, the readiest means herein to try our faith is by such main fundamental truths therein contained and plainly taught, upon which all other truths do in some sort depend and unto which they are to be reduced. Therefore, let us examine our consciences in these points:

1. Whether do we unfeignedly believe the mystery of the Trinity, the creation of the world, the fall of Adam, [and] the incarnation, death, resurrection, and ascension of Jesus Christ; that there shall be a rising again of all flesh from death to life [and] a general day of judgment; that there is a heaven, a hell, an everlasting life for some and an eternal death for othersome after this life; and such other

grounds of religion evidently contained in the Word of God and collected and proved by the same in our ordinary confessions of faith and catechisms.

2. More specially, whether we believe that the law of God (the sum whereof is contained in the Ten Commandments[1]) is a holy, perfect, and just law,[2] and such a law as God may justly bind every man to the obedience of every commandment therein contained, and whether we believe that he that perfectly keeps this law[3] is a blessed and happy man.[4]

3. Whether we believe that the breach of this law deserves everlasting death and condemnation[5] and that God in His justice may punish everlastingly in hell fire the breakers thereof.[6]

4. Whether we believe that all men living upon earth since the fall of Adam have broken this law and so are guilty of everlasting death[7] and that no man (by reason of the corruption of his will[8]) is now since the said fall able to keep this law.

5. Whether we believe that [we] ourselves in particular are grievous sinners and have deserved by our sins everlasting death and condemnation, and that it is a great misery to be a sinner, and a happiness to be free from sin.[9]

---

1. Matt. 22:40.
2. Rom. 7:12; 9:14–16.
3. Ps. 19:7; Deut. 6:2; 4:5.
4. Deut. 28:15.
5. 2 Thess. 1:9; Gal. 3:10; Rom. 6:23.
6. Rom. 9:13–14.
7. Rom. 3:10–12, 20–23; 5:12; Prov. 20:9.
8. Gen. 8:21; Rom. 7:7, 17.
9. Ps. 32:4; 40:12; 51:3–5; Neh. 1:7; Dan. 9:5–12; Ezra 9:6.

6. Whether we believe that God will punish everlastingly in hell fire a great part of the world for their sin, and that to the praise of His glorious justice.[10]

7. Whether we believe that neither [we] ourselves nor any man else by his own power, strength, or merit is able to free himself from this condemnation. And therefore, if there be no means out of ourselves to save us, that we also shall be in the number of those that shall be everlastingly condemned.[11]

8. Whether we believe that God will show grace and mercy to some sinners, freely saving, pardoning, and forgiving them without the least merit and desert[12] on their part.[13]

9. Whether we believe that all that are saved and pardoned of their sins are partakers of this mercy only through the merits of Jesus Christ, God and man, and that He merited the same by His death and blood-shedding upon the cross.[14]

10. Whether we believe that the merits of Christ are sufficient for the pardon and forgiveness of our own sins in particular.[15]

11. Whether we believe that all that are saved by Jesus Christ shall in this life (if they come to years of discretion) have the mystery of redemption revealed unto them in the preaching of the gospel, by means whereof they shall effectually be called out of the

---

10. Luke 19:27; 12:49; Matt. 7:13; Rom. 9:27; Prov. 16:4.
11. Rom. 3:23; 5:6, 12; 7:18–20.
12. *Desert*: deserving.
13. John 17:9; Dan. 9:7; Rom. 5:14; 9:22–23; Heb. 4:6.
14. Rom. 8:1; 7:24–25; 5:1–12; 3:28; Matt. 1:21.
15. John 1:12; 6:35; Matt. 9:2; Rom. 7:24–25; Isa. 1:18; Heb. 9:14.

world to faith and repentance;[16] that they shall testify the same by sorrow unfeigned for their sins past and [by] an endeavor carefully to lead a new life ever after and in a readiness to do Jesus Christ faithful service in His church, according to His will revealed in His Word;[17] and that after this life all such shall reign with Christ Jesus in all bliss and glory in heaven, for ever and ever.[18]

12. Whether we believe that all such as do believe and unfeignedly repent them of their sins and have a constant purpose to lead a new life, according to the will and Word of God, are in the number of them that shall be saved everlastingly.[19] And whether we judge and believe that it is a sin for any such person to despair of the mercy of God and not to repose trust and confidence therein.[20]

13. Whether we believe that all those persons are most vile and miserable that are not called to faith and repentance, and that they (most of all other) are most vile and wicked persons that contemn and despise or care not to use those means that God has ordained to bring them thereunto.[21]

14. Whether we believe that we are bound to use all the means we can for attaining faith and repentance, and whether we believe that in using the means we

---

16. Rom. 8:30–31; 1 Cor. 1:30; John 15:19; 17:6, 20–21.
17. Eph. 5:30; John 15:1; Ezek. 11:19; Acts 16:14; John 1:12; 2 Peter 1:5.
18. Matt. 25:34; Rev. 22:1–3; 2 Tim. 4:8.
19. John 3:36; 1 John 5:10.
20. John 3:18, 36.
21. Matt. 11:21–25; Heb. 2:3.

shall attain them.[22] And lastly, whether when we feel that we have in some measure obtained these graces we do believe that [we] ourselves in particular are of that number that shall be saved, or whether we do use all endeavor (at the least) and unfeignedly desire to believe the same.[23]

In these several points consist the substance and matter of the true Christian faith, every one of which is evidently revealed in the Word of God, so that those who are conversant in the same, if they do not willfully shut their eyes against the light, cannot but see them plainly set down therein. And upon these grounds and principles do all other truths in the Word of God (in some sort) depend, tending either to the confirmation or illustration of them, so that, if in the trial of ourselves we can find assuredly that we believe all and every of these points, and do our uttermost endeavor to believe them more and more, then verily our faith is sound, in regard of the main matter and substance thereof, though in divers other particulars (through our ignorance and corruption) it may be weak and unsound.

---

22. Matt. 7:7–8; 21:22; Mark 11:24; 2 Tim. 4:7–8; Luke 2:29; Job 19:25.

23. Mark 9:24; Luke 17:5; Matt. 5:6; Rev. 21:6.

CHAPTER 5

The Trial of Our Repentance

The second main grace that is in all those that are in grace and favor with God is repentance, the trial whereof is also a trial of our faith. That person whose heart is destitute hereof is as yet odious in God's sight and therefore a most unworthy partaker of this sacrament.

Repentance is an unfeigned hatred of all sin, arising especially from faith. As they that want [lack] faith want a mouth to eat the body and blood of Christ, so they that want repentance want an appetite and a stomach thereunto. For how can they hunger and thirst after the Lamb of God that takes away the sins of the world who have not this grace to repent them of their sins? And how can they thankfully and worthily eat the body and drink the blood of that Lamb which was sacrificed for their sin, that have no desire nor appetite thereunto?

The means, then, to try whether this repentance be in us or no is to make inquisition after the special signs and effects thereof. As,

1. Whether we do feel and perceive that we are grievous sinners, accuse and condemn ourselves from our

hearts for our sins, and acknowledge the just merit and desert of our sin.[1]

2. Whether we did come to the sense and feeling of our sin by the law of God, whether we love the same law the more by how much the more it discovers our sins, and whether also we love those means best that are most powerful and effectual to bring us unto the knowledge, sense, and feeling of our sins.[2]

3. Whether the more that we hear and believe the gospel (and in it the love and mercy of Jesus Christ toward sinners), the more we hate and forsake our sin.[3]

4. Whether we hate a sin as much or more in ourselves than in another, and whether we love another because of conscience he forbears to sin.

5. Whether we hate and strive against that sin that our nature is most disposed unto and that loves and haunts us most.

6. Whether the more that we have formerly sinned against God, and by our sins dishonored God, the more now we desire and endeavor to please God.[4]

7. Whether we do strive against not only great sins, such as are punished at Assizes and Sessions,[5] but also small sins such as are not punished, nor ever called in question, in the courts and consistories of men.[6]

---

1. Ps. 51:3–4; Dan. 9:7–8; 1 Cor. 11:31.
2. Rom. 3:20; 4:15; 7:7; Ps. 119:18, 143, 176.
3. Gal. 5:24; 1 John 3:9; Rom. 6:2–5.
4. Luke 7:47.
5. *Assizes and Sessions*: courts of law.
6. Gal. 5:9; 1 Thess. 5:22.

8. Whether we hate and abhor in ourselves not only those sins that are hateful and detestable in the eyes of men but even those also that men will account a grace and honor unto us to commit and for which they will recompense and reward us, when it shall be revealed to us, out of God's Word, that they are sins.[7]

9. Whether we hate sin principally because God hates it and forbids it, and not only, and especially, in respect of the curse and punishment or of the laws of men.

10. Whether we do not repent that we did no sooner repent, and whether we would for any worldly good be in that estate that we were in before our repentance.[8]

11. Whether we can instance in any special or particular sins that formerly we loved and delighted in, which now we hate and strive against.

12. Whether we do so much the more study and embrace the contrary virtues unto such sins as we now repent of by how much the more we have been formerly given unto them.

13. Whether we are not afraid that something that we love and affect should (by the Word of God) be discovered to be a sin, and whether we do not desire and pray that God would discover unto us all our sins, to the end that we may strive against them and forsake them.

14. Whether we do rejoice and unfeignedly thank God when anything that we take pleasure and delight in is discovered to be a sin.

---

7. Gen. 3:6–9.
8. Phil. 3:7–8.

15. Whether we esteem it a singular blessing of God that we have been, and are, crossed of God in those sins that our nature thirsts after, and that we have not had that opportunity and means of committing them which our corruption has desired.

16. Whether we do not hate but rather love him that dutifully, lovingly, and [in a] brotherly [manner] does admonish us of a manifest sin, especially if it be a minister of God.

CHAPTER 6

New Obedience and the Trial Thereof

One main and special effect and fruit of true repentance, and consequently of faith (without which our persons cannot be acceptable unto God), is new obedience. New obedience is a constant purpose to forsake all sin and an endeavor to obey God in all things for Christ's sake.[1] Every article[2] of our faith is an irresistible argument to prove that we owe this duty unto God. And if we believe them truly, they will move us—yea, force us—unto the same in some measure or other. The means to try whether this grace be in us or no is to examine our consciences in these points following:

1. Whether we desire and endeavor to know the will, pleasure, and commandment of God, that we might thereby frame ourselves to please God.[3] And whether we do (to this end) use the most likely and approved means to come to the knowledge thereof. And whether we rejoice in the knowledge thereof after we have attained unto it.

---

1. 1 Peter 4:2; 1:22; Rom. 6:15; Acts 23:1; Dan. 3:18.

2. *Article*: most likely a reference to the Thirty-Nine Articles of the Church of England.

3. 1 Thess. 5:21; Acts 17:11; Ps. 119:15.

2. Whether we are content to subject our own wills, reason, and affections unto God's revealed will, and do not exalt our own wisdom and will above His.[4]

3. Whether we labor to persuade ourselves that we shall lose nothing by yielding obedience to God's will and that it shall be worse for us for crossing His will in anything whatsoever—yea, that the more we lose by our obedience to God, the more we shall be sure to gain thereby.[5]

4. Whether we are not grieved when we meet with any lets and hindrances by means whereof we cannot do His will as we ought and would do it,[6] and whether we are unfeignedly sorry that we want strength and ability to do it as we would and should.

5. Whether we count it a grace, honor, and favor unto us that God would vouchsafe to command us any service, and whether we think nothing too base for us to do that He requires at our hands.[7]

6. Whether it be grievous unto us that others do not obey God and whether it be hateful unto us that another man should displease God to pleasure us.[8]

7. Whether we think all the service and duties that God requires of us, to be performed either to Himself or to our neighbor, to be less by many degrees than He has deserved at our hands, and whether, if He

---

4. Gal. 5:24; 1 Cor. 1:18–20; Matt. 26:39; Num. 22:19.
5. 1 Peter 4:12–19; Matt. 19:28–29; Phil. 1:29; Ps. 119:71; 1 Cor. 1:4; Rom. 5:3.
6. Rom. 7:24; 2 Cor. 12:8; Prov. 30:8–9.
7. Matt. 16:24.
8. Ps. 119:136.

should desire greater matters at our hand, we think ourselves bound to yield obedience unto them.[9]

8. Whether we account meanly and basely of our obedience and of the best service we can perform, or at any time have performed to God, as that which is of no value to merit the least grace and favor of Him.[10]

9. Whether it be a tediousness and vexation unto our souls to live in those places where we cannot have opportunity to serve and please God as we would and ought to do. And whether we love those places most where we have most means and opportunity to serve and honor God.[11]

10. Whether we love those persons most from whence we have most helps and encouragements to serve and please God.[12] And whether of all other persons we dislike them most that cross and hinder our obedience unto God and will not suffer us to perform those duties unto Him which we are able to do, and willingly would do, and which lay snares and stumbling blocks in our ways that we may not freely serve Him as we would.

11. Whether we desire to live no longer than that we may be able to do God some honor and service, and whether, every day more than another, the longer we live, we think ourselves bound, and endeavor to do better and better service unto God and to make Him amends for our negligent past, all the days of our life before.[13]

---

9. Rom. 9:3; Gen. 22:1–2.
10. Luke 18:13; Ps. 51:17; Isa. 66:2.
11. Ps. 120:5; 84:1–4; 27:4.
12. 1 Thess. 5:12.
13. Phil. 1:9–11.

CHAPTER 7

The Persons That Are to Make This Trial

Hitherto of the trial itself. The persons that are to make this trial are ourselves, upon ourselves: "Let a man therefore," says the apostle, "examine himself" [1 Cor. 11:28]. The reason whereof is evident: for it is not possible that another man should by trial find out what is in our hearts and consciences. For though another should use never so many experiments and try never so many conclusions upon us, yet may we through our hypocrisy and cunning dissimulation cozen[1] and delude him, though he were the wisest man and severest inquisitor in the world. Yea, our own hearts are so full of fraud and guile that if in this trial and examination of ourselves we do not proceed by a sound and sincere rule, we shall exceedingly cozen ourselves, and we shall conceit that that grace is in our hearts which was never in them in deed and truth.

Does not experience teach us that some persons have made great shows of piety, and more than an ordinary profession thereof, insomuch that they have seemed not only to others but out of doubt even to themselves to burn in zeal to some special truths and causes of Christ, who yet afterward have

---

1. *Cozen*: cheat, deceive.

proved detestable apostates and bloody and desperate persecutors of that in others which [they] themselves have professed?

The Lord seldom leaves His church without some notorious example or other of this kind, that we might the more narrowly try and examine the sincerity of our hearts and take heed [that] we be not deceived with shows and semblances of grace instead of substances.

This trial of ourselves does not exclude the trial that others (as far as they are able) are to make of us, especially our governors, teachers, and instructors, such as have the cure and charge of our souls, but it rather strengthens and confirms the same. For they who in singleness of heart shall once set themselves to this work shall find it of that difficulty that they will be glad of any furtherance and direction that they can get. For those trials and examinations that others use to make of us are but helps and directions [for] how we may (in the best manner) try and examine ourselves. Those, therefore, who are so ready to conclude from hence that others have nothing to do to examine them because they are here required to examine themselves might as well conclude that nobody else is to care for or do good to them, because they are to care for and do good for themselves.

But the truth is, such persons as are not willing that others should examine them do never purpose to examine themselves but are guilty to themselves of ignorance and gracelessness, and affect the same. Therefore, [they] had rather live and rot therein than discover it to others, though they might have help thereby. Indeed, if this were the end of such trials—to find out the defects, wants, and infirmities of our brethren, to the end that they may be drawn forth to punishment or that we might have matter of contempt or division against them— it were somewhat to except against it. But seeing the use and intent thereof is to find out what spiritual grace the person examined wants,[2] to the end that the best means might be used to supply the same, is it not strange that any should be found unwilling to submit unto the same, much more to judge it an injury and wrong? If a rich man should come to a poor man and in love and pity examine him of his estate, desiring to make known unto him what he wants (whether money, corn, or other provision for himself, his wife, and children) [and] promising to supply the same, were he not a strange man if being in extreme want—himself, wife, and children ready to starve with hunger—he should murmur and grudge at this rich man and ask what he had to do to examine him? Verily, thus it is with many poor, ignorant souls among us; the more they stand in need of spiritual relief, the less they can endure to be examined of their poverty and nakedness by those who are desirous to help and relieve them the best they can. But we may note hence,

1. That this is not sufficient to make a worthy receiver: that upon trial and examination made by others, he be found worthy. A man by wise and politic[3] carriage may so demean himself that even the best and holiest and most learned, after that they have sifted him to the uttermost, shall find no just matter of exception against him. And many bear this mind, that if they can so behave themselves as no man else can accuse them, though they be guilty to their own conscience of never so many corruptions, that then they are worthy enough of Christ and this sacrament and all other prerogatives of Christians. But the apostle teaches us here never to judge ourselves tried enough but when we are approved to our own

---

2. *Wants*: lacks.
3. *Politic*: prudent, discreet.

souls and consciences. For the strictest inquisitors may free and acquit us when our own consciences have a thousand capital crimes to arraign, convict, and condemn us of. Let us not, therefore, in the matter of our own worthiness so much rely upon the judgment of others, though it were of the best in the world, as of our own consciences, which are better able to judge of our own inward estate than all the world besides. But most judge themselves Christians worthy enough if no man else be able to lay any special unworthiness to their charge. But then the apostle would have sent us to others (and not to ourselves) to be tried and examined.

2. The duty of trying and examining a man's self is of use to the best of Christians. For many times none feel in themselves more want of graces than they do, [and] none are more dejected with the sense and feeling of their defects than they are. And many times they think they want those graces most with which their souls are most richly adorned.

And thus much of the first duty, which the apostle propounds as a special means to prevent the profaning of this sacrament.

CHAPTER 8

The Continuance in Trial till We Find That We Seek For

The other duty propounded by the apostle (but implicitly) is that we give not over trying and searching of ourselves until we find these graces in us. For the apostle requires of him that examines himself "That he eat of this bread, and drink of this cup" [1 Cor. 11:28].

What? Is he to do this whether in this search and trial he shall find any grace in himself or no? To what end, then, should a man make any such trial? This case is clear, that a man is not to receive this sacrament except after trial he find himself to be in the state of grace. But why does not the apostle put in this caution and exception?

1. Because he would thereby teach all Christians so long to continue the trial and examination of themselves until they have found in themselves (in some degree) the graces above specified.

2. To show that a man has not tried and examined himself in that manner which the Holy Ghost means until he has found in himself the graces aforesaid.

3. To teach that he that has this grace, but to search seriously within himself, shall in good time find these graces in himself.

It is the precise promise of our Savior: "Seek and you shall find" [Luke 11:5].

What an encouragement, then, ought this to be unto every one of us, to rifle and ransack our own souls, searching every corner of them as one would search for a mine of gold, seeing we are sure beforehand to find the graces we seek, and in and with them (which will be of more worth to us than a thousand worlds) a sealed pardon of the forgiveness of our sins—yea, sure evidences and indentures of a firm title to the kingdom of heaven. If a condemned man should be certified that if he did make diligent search he should without fail find the king's pardon, or if a needy beggar were informed that if he would seek and search narrowly in such a place he should be sure to find such treasures of gold and silver as would make him a rich man as long as he lived, would any man pity either the poverty of the one or the death of the other if they should refuse in those cases to take pains to search? Much less are such to be pitied that may find saving grace, if they will seek for it. Can there be a greater sign of a man that despises the grace of God than in such a case as this is—not to seek after it when a man may be sure to have it for the seeking after?

Here may we note, by the way, that the apostle does not only tie the duty of examination to the receiving of this sacrament but also the receiving of this sacrament to the duty of examination. Not that we should never examine ourselves but before the receiving of this sacrament, or upon this occasion only, but that doing it upon this occasion we should then after the doing of it receive, and not forsake, the Table of the Lord. These points following are plainly taught unto us by the apostle:

1. That the danger of receiving unworthily must not withhold us from receiving this sacrament but must make us so much the more studious to use the means of

worthy receiving the same. For the apostle does not say "Let a man therefore forbear to receive" but "Let a man therefore try and examine himself, and so let him eat" [1 Cor. 11:28], so that the more dangerous it is to receive unworthily, the more we must endeavor to be worthy receivers. And hence the apostle infers this duty from the danger aforesaid, as if he should say, "Every Christian stands bound to receive this sacrament. Yet seeing the danger of unworthy receiving is so great, our duty is the more carefully to study how we may be worthy receivers."

2. That all Christians which are bound to receive are bound to make this trial before they receive.

3. That after we have made this trial, it is a sin not to receive this sacrament.

CHAPTER 9

The Curse That Follows the Neglect of the Trial Aforesaid

Thus much of the duties necessary to the worthy receiving of this sacrament. The apostle furthermore urges and presses the church of Corinth (and us in them) to this duty:

1. In general, by showing the curse that they incur which without this trial do eat unworthily

2. In special, by showing what signs and tokens of that curse were among the Corinthians themselves.

The curse he first propounds and [then] secondly affixes the special ground and reason thereof.

The curse propounded is this: that a man, not trying and examining himself, eats and drinks unworthily, and therein and thereby "eateth and drinketh his own damnation" [1 Cor. 11:29]. That is, instead of receiving any spiritual food, they receive thereby (except the special mercy of God prevent it) that which will be a bane and poison to their souls. The bread and wine received shall be so far from being to them the body and blood of Christ that it shall be unto them as the sop was to Judas, a means in and by which Satan shall enter into them. They shall be so far from furthering their salvation thereby that if they had no other sin, that should be sin enough to pull upon their heads eternal condemnation.

If God should turn these elements of bread and wine (being unworthily received) unto a bodily bane and poison unto us, would it not make us fear and tremble how we received them, and to try and examine ourselves thoroughly before we presumed to receive the same? Surely, if upon our unworthy receiving our bowels and entrails should be in danger to rot within us, yet if no more evil than that should follow, it were nothing so fearful a matter as this is, to eat and drink our own damnation. As therefore we hate and abhor the damnation of our souls, we should hate and abhor the unworthy receiving of this sacrament, and love and embrace those means by which we may become worthy receivers thereof.

The ground of the curse is because such "do not discern the body of Christ" [1 Cor. 11:29]; that is, [they] make no difference between that food and those dainties which God prepares and offers in this sacrament—even the precious body and blood of our Savior Christ—and other ordinary meats and drinks, eating and devouring the bread and wine, never looking after nor regarding to eat and drink the body and blood of Christ exhibited thereby. What is this but to contemn Christ and His merits and to offer a foul indignity to God that prepares this feast? And how can they but endanger themselves to perish eternally that discern not nor look after that food by which they should live eternally?

CHAPTER 10

The Special Signs and Tokens of the Aforesaid Curse in the Church of Corinth

The apostle more specially shows the curse aforesaid by certain special signs and tokens thereof in the church of Corinth— namely, certain special judgments of God that at that time were inflicted upon divers persons in and of that church.

These judgments were bodily afflictions of divers sorts and degrees. Some were smitten with one kind of infirmity and some with another, and some with death itself. "For this cause," says the apostle, "many of you are weak, and sick, and many sleep" (1 Cor. 11:30). Hence we learn

1. That we ought in a special manner to reverence and religiously use those ordinances of God, the profanation whereof He marks and brands with particular visible judgments. God's mere threatening of death after this life should be enough to terrify Christians from the abuse of any of His ordinances. Much more, then, should they move us when (as so many seals and sacraments thereof) He shall annex thereunto sensible[1] plagues and punishments in this life. We cannot but see that many plagues and judgments are gone forth from the throne of God into the

---

1. *Sensible*: perceived by the senses.

world—yea, into the church; yea, into many of our houses and upon our own persons. Neither do we see the judgments only, but we might see also (if we did not willfully shut our eyes) for what particular sins God inflicts many of them. Who is it that cannot see that so many plagues and vengeances have fallen and do yet lie upon such and such men for their murders, thefts, adulteries, treasons, perjuries, drunkenness, and so on? And yet neither the sight of these judgments, no, nor the sense and feeling of some of them in our own persons will serve to restrain us from those sins. But in the midst of so many judgments these sins abound and, as it were, triumph over them.

2. We may learn that the unworthy and profane receivers of this sacrament do not only eat and drink therein a spiritual judgment that hypocrites and carnal men do not so much care for, but even bodily judgments also, so that it may prove in the end and effect no better than a very bane and poison unto our bodies and a means of many grievous diseases, yea, and of untimely death. For so it proved (we see) to some of these Corinthians, and we can plead no special privilege. The more, therefore, that we may love our bodily lives and health, the more let us make conscience of the former duties. These kinds of judgments here mentioned are no strangers among us; yea, the hand of God in this kind has lain a long time heavy upon us, and though we cannot precisely say (as the apostle here does) that for this very cause some of us are afflicted with this disease and some with that, and so many with the pestilence, and so on, yet having such a precedent set before us in the Word of God of such a sin punished with such judgments, it being too apparent that not only the same

sin does reign among us but that also the same judgments lie in great weight and measure upon us, we have just cause to fear that among others, this very sin is one cause thereof. And therefore, in seeking to remove these judgments, let us have a special care among other sins to reform this.

3. So oft as any of us are guilty unto ourselves of irreverent and unworthy receiving of this sacrament, and the more free we have been withal from any of these judgments, in the greater danger we should fear ourselves to be. For we are indebted so many deaths and sicknesses to the Lord, which (except we prevent betimes with true repentance) we shall be sure to pay with the interest, either in this life or in another. For the Lord as much hates this sin in us as in the Corinthians and will be sure at some time or other, by one means or other, to punish it severely. And the more He defers to punish it, the more severely He will do it when He takes the rod once into His hands. Let us then in the fear of God take heed how in this case we too much abuse the patience and long-suffering of God; patience wounded becomes fury.

For the further enforcing of this, the apostle shows, first, the justice of God in this curse of His, and second, His mercy.

First, His justice, in that He had not thus sharply judged them if they had judged themselves. "For," says he, "if we would judge ourselves, we should not be judged" (1 Cor. 11:31). As though he should say, "We may thank ourselves for these and such like judgments that lie upon us, and can no way blame God for them. For it is just with Him, the best of us being so sinful as we are, that when we will not judge and condemn ourselves, we should be in such a manner judged and condemned by Him." Hence we may learn

    i. That the best means to prevent any judgment of God, whether temporal or eternal, is to accuse, arraign, judge, and condemn ourselves. And contrarily, the surest way to pull down all sorts of judgments upon ourselves is to justify ourselves and to glory in the merits of our own righteousness.

Would we then in [a] most effectual manner prevent sickness, shame, [and] death? Let us examine ourselves and search what sins are in us, and pass the severest sentence of condemnation against ourselves that may be. The more (if it be done unfeignedly) we shall condemn ourselves, the more the Lord will justify us.

    i. The due trial and examination of a man's self, and the judging and condemning of a man's self, do necessarily follow one upon another. Otherwise there is no good coherence of these words with the former.

He, then, that shall carefully and conscionably examine himself shall be sure to find matter enough in himself to judge and condemn himself for.

He does most worthily eat and drink this sacrament that shall discern in himself most matter of judgment and condemnation. And none [are] more unworthy receivers thereof than those that can find nothing in themselves to judge and condemn themselves for.

Second, the apostle shows the mercy of God toward them herein: that these judgments (unto them that can make right use of them) are but fatherly and loving chastisements and instructions to keep them from the common condemnation of the world. "But," says he, "whilst we are judged, we are chastened [or nurtured and instructed] of the Lord, because we should not be condemned with the world" [1 Cor. 11:32].

As if he should have said, "You are notwithstanding to behold God's mercy toward you, shining in this justice of His. For He does this not out of any hatred He bears to any of you that are humbled under this hand of His, and can make a good use thereof, but as a loving and dear father chastens and corrects his child when he sees him in any fault, not that he might be avenged of him but only thereby to terrify him and keep him from such courses as might bring him to the gibbet or gallows or any other such shameful end. So God exercises you with these temporal chastisements that thereby He might keep and restrain you from following such courses as might bring you (with the rest of the wicked world) to eternal damnation."

The consideration hereof should not embolden us to be the less careful of the former duties but rather to make more conscience of them. For howsoever those who receive this sacrament unworthily do not so eat and drink their own damnation that there is no means or hope of mercy left unto them, being fallen into this sin, and though these temporal judgments that God inflicts as signs and tokens that therein they eat and drink their own damnation are to some persons the effects of God's love and the means to save them from that damnation, yet cursed and desperate must their state needs be that shall in such a manner abuse so great a mercy and love of God; yea, these temporary judgments do so far forth only proceed from His love as they are sanctified unto us and made holy instruments, in and through them to see and behold what an odious and damnable sin it is to receive unworthily. And so they become a good means to make us repent of it and forsake that sin. In others they are but the forerunners of eternal punishment. Thus much for our help and direction, that we may be worthy and fruitful receivers of this sacrament.

The Lord for His mercy's sake pardon our former wants herein and move our hearts to the careful performance of all these duties, that so we may not only avoid the judgments which unworthy receivers are in danger to fall into but that we receiving these mysteries worthily may in and by them receive the assurance of that grace and mercy which is shadowed and represented by them, even the full and perfect redemption of our bodies and souls through the sacrifice of Christ's body and His most precious blood shed upon the cross. Amen.

PART 3

A Preparation to the Receiving of Christ's Body and Blood

A Brief Form of Examination

A Brief Form of Examination

Question 1: *What is a sacrament?*
Answer: A mystical sign ordained of God to represent and seal to the worthy receiver salvation by Christ Jesus.

    Matt. 28:19; 1 Cor. 11:23; Gen. 17:7; Rom. 4:11

Question 2: *Who is Christ Jesus?*
Answer: The eternal and only begotten Son of God and our only Savior.

    Matt. 3:17; Rom. 1:3; John 1:14; 1 Tim. 2:5; Heb. 2:17

Question 3: *What is God?*
Answer: An infinite and eternal Majesty, the Creator and Governor of the world.

    Ps. 139:7; 1 Kings 8:27; Isa. 44:6; Ps. 90:2; Gen. 1:1; Ps. 19; Zech. 9:10; Prov. 15:3

Question 4: *How many Gods are there?*
Answer: Only one in three persons.

    John 17:3; Ex. 20:2; 1 Cor. 8:6; 1 John 5:7

Question 5: *Which be those three persons?*
Answer: God the Father, God the Son, and God the Holy Ghost.

    Matt. 28:19

Question 6: *How is Christ our Savior?*
Answer: By redeeming us from hell and purchasing heaven
for us.
> Matt. 20:28; John 3:14–15

Question 7: *What is heaven?*
Answer: A place of everlasting joy and glory.
> Matt. 25:34; Luke 16:22; 1 Cor. 2:9; Rev. 21:23; 22:1–2

Question 8: *What is hell?*
Answer: A place of everlasting torment.
> Luke 16:23; Rev. 20:10; Matt. 25:46; Isa. 30:33

Question 9: *How came we in danger of hell?*
Answer: By sin.
> Rom. 5:10, 12; Gen. 2:17

Question 10: *What is sin?*
Answer: A breach of God's commandments.
> 1 John 3:4; Rom. 7:7; Gal. 3:10

Question 11: *What are those commandments?*
Answer: "God spake," and so on.
> [Ex. 20:1–17]

Question 12: *Have all men broken these commandments?*
Answer: Yea, all without exception.
> Rom. 3:9–10, 23; Gal. 3:22

Question 13: *Does every breach of these commandments deserve
everlasting torment in hell?*
Answer: Yea, verily.
> Rom. 6:23; Gal. 3:10; Deut. 27:26

Question 14: *How many sorts of sin are there?*
Answer: Two: original and actual.

Question 15: *What is original sin?*
Answer: A corruption of nature, whereby we are inclined to the breach of all God's commandments.
> Ps. 51:5; Rom. 7:14, 18; 8:7

Question 16: *Is this corruption in all?*
Answer: Yea.
> Gen. 8:21; Rom. 5:12

Question 17: *How came we to the same?*
Answer: By the fall of Adam, our first father.
> Rom. 5:12; 1 Cor. 15:22

Question 18: *How did he fall?*
Answer: By eating of the fruit of a tree that God had forbidden upon pain of death.
> Gen. 3:6

Question 19: *What is actual sin?*
Answer: A particular breach of God's commandments—in thought, word, and deed—arising from original corruption.
> Gen. 6:5; Gal. 5:19; Eph. 2:3; Rom. 3:13

Question 20: *By what means has Christ redeemed us from hell and purchased heaven for us?*
Answer: By fulfilling the law and dying for us.
> Phil. 2:8; Matt. 5:17; 3:15; Rev. 5:9; Heb. 9:15

Question 21: *How could the Son of God, being God, perform this?*
Answer: He took upon Him our nature and so became God and man in one person.
> John 1:14; Rom. 9:5

Question 22: *How did He take our nature upon Him?*

Answer: He was miraculously conceived by the Holy Ghost in the womb of a virgin.

> Isa. 7:14; Matt. 1:20; Luke 1:35; John 1:14

Question 23: *What death did He die for us?*

Answer: An accursed death upon the cross.

> Matt. 27:35; Gal. 3:13

Question 24: *Was there no other way to save us?*

Answer: No, verily.

> Acts 4:12; Rom. 7:23–24

Question 25: *Does our Savior Christ, then, continue still under death?*

Answer: No, but He rose again the third day and ascended into heaven, and there sits in all glory at the right hand of His Father, making intercession for us.

> John 20; Matt. 28; Acts 1; 2:31; 1 Cor. 15; Mark 16:19

Question 26: *Shall all men be saved by Christ?*

Answer: No, but such only (if they be of years) as by faith and repentance become new men.

> Eph. 3:17; Col. 2:12; John 3:16; 1:12; 6:35; Acts 13:39; 20:21; Mark 1:4, 15

Question 27: *What is faith?*

Answer: A confidence in the merits of Christ only for salvation.

> Acts 16:31; John 1:12

Question 28: *What is repentance?*

Answer: An unfeigned hatred of all sin for Christ's sake.

> Acts 3:19; 2 Cor. 7:10–11; Matt. 3:7, 8, 10

Question 29: *By what means do we attain unto faith and repentance ordinarily?*
Answer: By the preaching of God's Word.
> Eph. 1:13; Rom. 10:17

Question 30: *What is God's Word?*
Answer: His revealed will contained in the writings of the prophets and apostles.
> 2 Tim. 3:15–16; 2 Peter 1:20; 3:2; Luke 24:27

Question 31: *What were those prophets and apostles?*
Answer: Men that wrote by divine inspiration.
> 2 Tim. 3:16; 2 Peter 1:21

Question 32: *What be the parts of God's Word?*
Answer: The law and the gospel.

Question 33: *What is the law?*
Answer: That part of God's Word which shows the cursed estate that all men are in by reason of sin.
> Gal. 3:19; Rom. 3:10

Question 34: *What is the gospel?*
Answer: That part of God's Word which shows how we are freed from that curse by Jesus Christ.
> Acts 16:30–31; John 3:16; Mark 1:1

Question 35: *Where is God's Word ordinarily preached?*
Answer: In the churches of Christ.

Question 36: *What are the churches of Christ?*
Answer: Holy assemblies joining ordinarily and [in an] orderly [manner] together in the worship of God.
> 1 Cor. 1:2; 2 Cor. 1:1; Titus 1:5

Question 37: *Wherein consists the worship of God?*

Answer: In hearing the Word, receiving the sacraments, and praying.

> Matt. 28:18–19; Acts 15:21; 1 Tim. 2:1; 1 Cor. 11:23

Question 38: *By whom is the Word of God preached?*

Answer: By the ministers of Christ.

> Eph. 4:11–12

Question 39: *Who are the ministers of Christ?*

Answer: Such as having gifts given them of God are set apart by the church to preach the Word, administer the sacraments, and to be the mouth of the people unto God in prayer.

> Heb. 5:4; Rom. 10:15

Question 40: *Do all attain unto faith and repentance unto whom the Word is preached?*

Answer: No, but those only in whom God of His special grace works the same by His own Spirit.

> Acts 16:14; Eph. 2:8; Rom. 10:17

Question 41: *Who are those?*

Answer: His elect.

> Acts 13:48

Question 42: *What are they?*

Answer: Such as from all eternity He has purposed to save by Jesus Christ.

> Rom. 9:22–23; 1 Thess. 5:9

Question 43: *Is there anything in them above others that moves God hereunto?*

Answer: Nothing in the world but His own mere good will and pleasure.

> Eph. 1:4–5, 11; Rom. 9:18–22

Question 44: *Why does He vouchsafe this grace to some?*
Answer: For the praise of His glorious mercy.
> Rom. 9:23

Question 45: *Why does He deny this grace to other some?*
Answer: For the praise of His glorious justice.
> Rom. 9:22

Question 46: *What shall be the estate of those that attain unto faith and repentance?*
Answer: They shall in this life daily grow and increase therein.
> Ps. 1:3

Question 47: *By what special means shall they grow and increase therein?*
Answer: By the due use of the Word, sacraments, and prayer.

Question 48: *But what shall their estate be after this life?*
Answer: Their souls shall go to heaven and there remain till the last day, and then both body and soul shall be united again, and both shall continue with Christ in all glory in heaven for ever and ever.

Question 49: *What is the last day?*
Answer: A day of general judgment, wherein all flesh shall be raised from death and receive final sentence from God for that which they have done in this life.
> Matt. 25:31–46

Question 50: *What sentence shall pass upon those that repent and believe in Christ?*
Answer: They shall be acquit[ted] from all their sins and received into everlasting glory.
> Matt. 25:34

Question 51: *What sentence shall pass upon the rest?*
Answer: All their sins shall be discovered and laid to their charges, and they shall be cast body and soul into hell fire.

> Matt. 25:41–46

Question 52: *How many sacraments are there?*
Answer: Two: baptism and the Lord's Supper.

> Matt. 28:19; 1 Cor. 11:23–26

Question 53: *What is baptism?*
Answer: A mystical washing with water, in the name of the Father, Son, and Holy Ghost.

> Titus 3:5; Matt. 28:19

Question 54: *What does water especially signify?*
Answer: The blood of Christ.

> Eph. 5:26

Question 55: *What does the washing signify?*
Answer: That we are freed from the guilt of sin and sanctified by the merits of Christ, especially by His death and blood-shedding.

> Eph. 5:26; Mark 1:4; Acts 2:38; Titus 3:5; 1 Cor. 6:11

Question 56: *Who are to be admitted to baptism?*
Answer: All that truly profess faith and repentance, and their infants.

> Acts 2:38–39; 8:37; Gen. 17:7; 1 Cor. 7:14

Question 57: *Who are these?*
Answer: Such as do nothing that is manifestly contrary thereunto in the knowledge of men, or if they have done any thing, give good signs of special repentance for the same.

Question 58: *How oft are they to be baptized?*
Answer: Only once.

Question 59: *When are they to be baptized?*
Answer: As soon as they can be admitted thereto by the church where they are called to live.
> Acts 2:41; 8:36; 10:47

Question 60: *What is the Supper of the Lord?*
Answer: A mystical communion in breaking and eating of bread and drinking of wine in special remembrance of Christ.
> Matt. 26:26; 1 Cor. 10:16

Question 61: *What does the bread and wine signify?*
Answer: The body and blood of Christ.
> 1 Cor. 10:16

Question 62: *What does the breaking of the bread signify?*
Answer: Those pains He endured in soul and body for our salvation, especially upon the cross.
> 1 Cor. 11:24

Question 63: *What does the eating of the bread and drinking of the wine signify?*
Answer: That by virtue of His merits (especially of His death and blood-shedding) applied to us by faith we are not only freed from eternal death in hell but shall live with Him in heaven for ever and ever.

Question 64: *Who are to be admitted to the receiving of this sacrament?*
Answer: All that, having been baptized, continue in the true profession of faith and repentance.
> 1 Cor. 11:27–29

Question 65: *How oft are they to receive the same?*
Answer: As oft as it may conveniently be administered in that church in which they have calling to live.
> Acts 2:42; 20:7

Question 66: *Who are worthy receivers of this sacrament?*
Answer: Such as bring a holy appetite thereunto.
> Matt. 5:6

Question 67: *What is that appetite?*
Answer: A spiritual hungering and thirsting after Christ Jesus and His merits.

Question 68: *Whence does this appetite arise?*
Answer: From a sense of the weakness of our faith and repentance, and a desire to have them strengthened.
> Acts 2:37–42

Question 69: *How may we come to this true sense?*
Answer: By preparing ourselves beforehand thereunto.

Question 70: *How are we to prepare ourselves?*
Answer: By examining the sincerity of our faith and repentance by the special fruits thereof.
> 1 Cor. 11:28

Question 71: *What are they?*
Answer: A constant and conscionable care to use all means for the getting and increasing of them, and a resolute purpose and endeavor to obey God in all things for Christ's sake.

Question 72: *What if we be unworthy receivers of the sacrament?*
Answer: We shall then eat and drink our own judgment.
> 1 Cor. 11:27, 29

Question 73: *What if we contemn or neglect to receive this sacrament?*
Answer: We therein declare that we contemn or neglect that which is signified thereby and offered therein.

> 1 Cor. 11:29

Question 74: *What if we receive the same worthily?*
Answer: We shall receive thereby Christ Himself, and in Him more and more assurance of our salvation.

> 1 Cor. 10:16

Question 75: *What if we shall be unjustly put from this communion?*
Answer: God in this case will accept our will for the deed.

FINIS

The Doctrine of Communicating Worthily in the Lord's Supper

Delivered by Way of Question and Answer
for the More Familiar Instruction of the Simple

by Arthur Hildersham

To the Reader

Good Reader,

After I had yielded to the publishing of mine own poor meditations upon 1 Corinthians 11:23,[1] there came to my hands in writing this ensuing treatise, written some years since by a godly and faithful pastor for the direction of his own people in the worthy receiving of the sacrament of the Lord's Supper, at what time he was first called unto them.

In the perusal whereof, I being in myself well persuaded of the fullness and perspicuity of that doctrine of preparation which it propounds to entreat of, the orderly method of every part thereof, the plain and familiar handling of the matter, and that it did supply many needful points of instruction that are wanting in mine own treatise, I was earnest with the author to give me leave to publish the same and to adjoin it as an ornament and help unto mine, which with much importunity at length I have obtained. Though in the hard and just conceit he entertains of it, he suffers it in this sort, as you see, to come abroad as a Child of the Earth, without any name from whom it is descended.[2]

---

1. William Bradshaw is referring to his own treatise on the Lord's Supper, published initially as *A Direction for the Weaker Sort of Christians Showing in What Manner They May Be Prepared to the Worthy Receiving of the Sacrament of the Bodie and Blood of Christ,* and then as *A Preparation to the Receiving of the Sacrament of Christ's Body and Blood.*

2. This sentence appears in the 1609 edition but not in the 1617 edition. Bradshaw is explaining that Hildersham had such a low opinion of his own work that he stipulated that it should be published

For the spiritual good that you shall receive thereby, bless the Lord and pray for the author, that God would restore him again to that former liberty in his church which heretofore to the glory of God and the comfort of many a Christian soul he has enjoyed.[3]

Yours in the Lord,
    W[illiam]. B[radshaw].

---

anonymously. By the later date, his authorship is so well known that this sentence and the anonymity were no longer appropriate; Hildersham's initials, though not his full name, appear on the 1617 title page.

3. At the time of Bradshaw's writing, Hildersham had been deprived of his vicarage at Ashby because of his ceremonial nonconformity.

The Doctrine of Communicating Worthily in the Lord's Supper

Question 1:[1] *How many things are required of those who would receive the sacrament of the Lord's Supper to their comfort?*

Answer: Three:

1. A diligent and careful preparation of themselves before they come to receive it

2. A reverent and attentive disposition of body and mind in the receiving of it

3. An unfeigned endeavor to feel and find in themselves the fruit of it after they have received it

Question 2: *What is that preparation that is required of everyone that would receive this sacrament to his comfort?*

Answer: Everyone (even such as have made best proceedings in religion) before he presumes to come to the Lord's Supper must sequester himself from all other business that might any way distract him. Then he must carefully set his whole mind and heart upon this work that he is to go about, taking some time to examine himself whether those things be in him that may make him a worthy receiver of this holy sacrament.

---

1. In the original the questions are not numbered. They have been added for ease of reference.

Question 3: *What reasons may be given to show the necessity of this so careful an examination and preparation of ourselves before this sacrament?*

Answer:

1. Such is the untowardness and corruption of our hearts that we are unfit to do any special service to God until we have taken some pains to prepare ourselves thereunto.

2. There is no part of His service before which the Lord has so strictly enjoined this preparation as before the receiving of this sacrament.[a] Before the Passover (which was in substance the same with this sacrament, and in the place whereof this was ordained by Christ), the Lord did not only command[b] that the lamb should be taken out of the flock three days before it was to be sacrificed (that His people might thereby be admonished to employ themselves during that time in fitting of themselves unto that service),[c] but also He enjoined them a special preparation before they came unto it. And the apostle [Paul] affirms of this sacrament that even they that are believers may and shall certainly receive it unworthily if they do not examine and judge themselves before they come.[d]

3. The extreme danger that he casts himself into that receives it unworthily should make every man afraid to come rashly, irreverently, or unpreparedly unto it.

[a] Ex. 19:10; 20.8, 1 Sam. 16.5, Joel 2.15–16, Job 11:13; Ps. 108:1; Eccles. 5:1; 2 Chron. 12:14
[b] Ex. 12:3–6
[c] 2 Chron. 35:6
[d] 1 Cor. 11:27–31

Question 4: *How may their danger appear to be so great that receive this sacrament unworthily?*

Answer: In eating of this bread and drinking of this wine, they shall eat and drink the judgment and curse of God.[a]

[a] 1 Cor. 11:29–34

Question 5: *By what judgments has God been wont to punish such as have profaned or irreverently used this or any other of His sacraments?*

Answer:

1. Sometimes by corporal and outward plagues, as He did those who in the days of Samuel used the ark without due reverence.[a] And those in the days of Hezekiah who went to the Passover not being sanctified and prepared thereunto, according to the law.[b] And those among the Corinthians who went to the Lord's Table before they had examined and judged themselves.[c]

2. Sometimes He punishes them as He did Judas (who with an evil and impenitent heart presumed to receive the Passover), by stripping them of those beginnings of grace they had received, hardening them, and making them unable to repent.[d] So as after they have received, they become twofold more the children of hell than they were before.

[a] 1 Sam. 5:6, 7, 9, 11, 12; 6:19
[b] 2 Chron. 30:17–18
[c] 1 Cor. 11:30
[d] John 13:27

Question 6: *What is the cause why the Lord is wont to be so severe in punishing the irreverent and unworthy receiving of this sacrament?*

Answer: Because the unworthy receiver is guilty of the body and blood of Christ.[a]

   [a] 1 Cor. 11:27

Question 7: *How can that be, seeing he receives it not, but the outward signs only?*

Answer: Because he discerns not the Lord's body, nor judges and esteems so highly and reverently of this His holy ordinance (whereby the same is represented and offered unto us) as he ought, but accounts it as common bread and wine, which the wicked as well as the godly have title unto.[a] This is far greater dishonor and contempt done to God than could be done to any king if his picture or [coat of] arms that hang up in some public place should be spat upon, or pulled down, or broken and trampled on by any of his subjects.

   [a] 1 Cor. 11:29

Question 8: *What use are we to make of this that has been said, touching the necessity of preparing ourselves aright before we come to the Lord's Table?*

Answer: First, that therefore the minister and church must do that which lies in them to keep from this sacrament all such as are unworthy and unprepared.[a]

   [a] 2 Chron. 23:19; 35:6; Jer. 15:19; Matt. 7:6; 1 Cor. 5:2, 7, 13

Question 9: *Why so?*

Answer: Because else they consent to the great dishonor that the unworthy receiver does unto God[a] and unto the certain peril that he casts his own soul into,[b] and so make themselves liable to that plague whereby God has been wont to punish whole congregations that have willingly tolerated so great an abuse.[c]

[a] 1 Sam. 2:29
[b] Lev. 19:17; Jude 23
[c] 1 Cor. 11:30; 5:2, 6

Question 10: *Is then the minister also bound to examine such as he admits unto this sacrament, and not to receive indifferently all that shall offer themselves?*

Answer: He is. For if at all other times he must be diligent to know the estate of his flock,[a] that he may accordingly be able to divide the Word of truth aright unto them[b] and give them their portion of meat in due season,[c] then much more must he be careful to know them at that time when he is to admit them to this holy sacrament.

[a] Prov. 27:23; Jer. 6:27; Acts 20:28; Phil. 2:19; 1 Thess. 3:5
[b] 2 Tim. 2:15
[c] Luke 12:42

Question 11: *Must then the people also be willing to have their lives looked into, and their knowledge examined by their pastor, and to make known unto him their spiritual estate, that so with comfort and boldness he may admit them?*

Answer: Yes, verily. For

1. Seeing God required of those that were to be baptized (being at the years of discretion) that they should first make known unto the congregation or minister their faith and repentance, He does surely every whit as much require this of those that are to come to the Lord's Supper.[a]

2. Every Christian is bound to acknowledge his pastor his superior in all matters that belong to God's worship and

to his own soul,[b] and therein to obey him and submit himself to his direction in the Lord.[c] So is he then especially to show his obedience to this ordinance of God when he intends to be a partaker of this sacrament, because there is no one action of the ministry wherein the necessity and dignity of that function is more set forth and commended by the Lord unto His church than in the administration of the sacraments that is committed unto them.[d] Neither is there any time wherein it more behooves his pastor to inquire into his estate than when he is to admit him unto the Lord's Table.

[a] Matt. 3:6; Acts 8:37
[b] 1 Tim. 2:12; Heb. 7:7
[c] Deut. 17:11–12; 1 Thess. 5:12–13; Heb. 13:17
[d] Matt. 3:14–15

Question 12: *But if they that are notoriously unworthy be (through the negligence of the church and pastor) admitted to the sacrament, can that deprive the faithful that receive with them of the benefit and comfort of the sacrament? Or ought they for that cause to keep themselves from it?*

Answer: No, for

1. No man's sin can defile another or make God's promise or sacrament of none effect unto him that is neither any way accessory unto it nor has power and authority to keep him from the sacrament.[a]

2. The holy apostles and our Savior Himself did communicate in the service of God with those assemblies wherein there were many notoriously wicked.[b]

3. If it had been so, the apostle [Paul] would have required every man not only to examine himself but all those with whom he is to receive.[c]

[a] Ezek. 18:20; Gal. 6:5
[b] Luke 2:22, 41; 24:53; Acts 21:26
[c] 1 Cor. 11:28

Question 13: *Makes it then nothing to our comfort what they are with whom we do communicate?*

Answer: Yes, we should desire to receive with them of whose holy profession and godly life we are well persuaded.

Question 14: *Why so?*

Answer:

1. Because in this sacrament we profess ourselves to be fellow members as with the whole church of Christ, so especially with those Christians with whom we do receive, and that we seek also and desire to be confirmed in that communion and to become more and more like unto them, both in faith and conversation.[a]

2. Because both our love and zeal may be better kindled and stirred up by the prayers and examples of such as we know to be godly than either by the wicked or such as we know not at all.[b]

   [a] 1 Cor. 10:17
   [b] Matt. 18:19–20; Phil. 3:17; Rom. 1:11–12

Question 15: *What other use is to be made of this doctrine, touching the necessity of preparing ourselves aright before we come to this sacrament?*

Answer: That everyone should be careful to examine himself and not rest in the approbation of the minister or church.[a]

   [a] 1 Cor. 11:28; Gal. 4:6

Question 16: *Why so?*

Answer:

1. Because a man may have a most wicked heart, and yet seem a good man to the church, and be guilty also of many gross crimes that are unknown to his pastor.[a]

2. Though a man live so as his pastor may discern just cause to doubt that he is not worthy (and consequently cannot admit him without grief), yet may not he refuse him until he be evidently able to convict him of some such thing as may prove him unworthy.[b]

3. It may so fall out that though a man's crime be public and apparent,[c] yet his pastor may want power to keep him from the sacrament.[2]

[a] John 13:24, 28
[b] Deut. 13:14; 17:4
[c] Matt. 18:17

Question 17: *As you have shown the necessity of preparation and the danger of such as receive unworthily, so tell me, who may be accounted worthy to come to the Lord's Table?*

Answer: As no man can deserve to receive Christ and all His merits, so can none deserve to be admitted to the Lord's Table, wherein the same are represented and offered unto him. But all that through God's free grace are made meet and fit to receive it[a] and come with such hearts as it beseems[3] men to bring to so holy and heavenly a banquet[b] are (in God's gracious acceptation) accounted worthy to come unto it.[c]

[a] Luke 3:8
[b] 1 Thess. 2:12; cf. Col. 1:12
[c] Rev. 3:4; cf. Luke 20:35

---

2. In the Church of England at this time, ministers were legally only allowed to exclude the notoriously wicked from Communion.

3. *Beseems*: is seemly, becomes.

Question 18: *Tell me, then, what are those special graces that are necessarily required for the making of us fit to come to the Lord's Table and that by diligent examination we must labor to find in ourselves?*

Answer: There are six in number:

1. A sincere and right desire of it
2. Knowledge
3. Faith
4. Repentance
5. Newness of life
6. Love

Question 19: *To handle these in order, tell me first what you mean by this sincere and right desire of the sacrament, without which you say none can come worthily unto it.*

Answer: We must find in ourselves an unfeigned and earnest desire unto it, and come unto it with a willing mind and a holy appetite and delight.[a]

[a] 1 Chron. 28:9; Ps. 110:3; 2 Cor. 8:10–11; 9:7; Luke 22:15; Acts 8:36

Question 20: *How may this sincere and right desire of this sacrament be discerned?*

Answer: When it arises from the serious consideration of these three things (which are the only reasons that should move us to come to the Lord's Supper)—namely,

1. The necessity of this sacrament

2. The great benefits that are to be received by it

3. The present need that we ourselves do stand in, of all those helps that the Lord in this sacrament has provided for us

Question 21: *How may the conscience of a man be persuaded of the necessity of this sacrament?*

Answer: By considering that this is a part of God's worship, which was ordained by Christ Himself even in the same night that He was betrayed. And that He did not only ordain it and first administer it Himself but also gave commandment to His disciples (who did represent the whole church, of which they were to be the master builders) to take, to eat and drink it, yea to do that often which was done in the first institution thereof, in remembrance of Him.[a] So that though[4] there were no benefit or comfort to be found in it, yet were we bound, in obedience to this ordinance and commandment of Christ, to come unto it.

[a] 1 Cor. 11:24–25

Question 22: *But seeing you have said that the consideration of the benefits that are to be received by it is another reason whereby we should be moved to desire it, tell me what benefits are those that a Christian may receive by this sacrament?*

Answer:

1. Whereas every Christian is bound not only to believe but also to take all good occasions of professing openly his faith and religion,[a] as being glad to wear the livery and badge of his heavenly Lord and Master, the receiving of the sacrament is one special means ordained of God whereby we are to make public profession that we are true believers and servants of God.[b]

2. Whereas every Christian, out of the sense and experience he has of his own proneness to apostasy,[c] should by all good means bind himself to continue in the faith and obedience of Christ,[d] the receiving of this sacrament is

4. *Though*: even if.

ordained of God to be as a solemn seal and vow whereby we bind ourselves (as strongly as by an oath) to continue in the faith and obedience of Christ and unity of His church.

3. Whereas every Christian is bound to use all good means whereby his faith may be quickened, confirmed, and increased in him, the receiving of this sacrament is a principal means that God has ordained for the reviving, strengthening, and increasing of our faith.[e]

[a] Isa. 44:5; Ps. 40:9–10; Matt. 10:32; John 12:42, 44; Rom. 10:10
[b] Ex. 13:9; Gen. 17:11; 1 Cor. 10:16, 21. For this cause Hezekiah so earnestly exhorts all God's people to come to the Passover (2 Chron. 30:1, 5) and calls this a turning to the Lord and renewing [of] their covenant with Him (2 Chron. 30:6, 8). For this cause it is said they kept it unto the Lord (2 Chron. 30:1; 35:1). This was one cause why Christ received the sacraments (Matt: 3:15; Mark 14:12).
[c] Deut. 29:10, 12; 2 Chron. 15:12, 14; Neh. 9:38; 10:28–29; Ps. 119:106
[d] Ex. 13:9; Matt. 28:19; Gal. 5:3; 1 Cor. 10:2
[e] 1 Cor. 16:13; 1 Thess. 5:19–20; 2 Peter 3:18

Question 23: *How may that appear?*

Answer: Because a singular promise of grace, and part of that covenant which God has made with us in Christ, is in a most comfortable manner taught and applied and confirmed to us by this sacrament.

Question 24: *What is that promise of grace which is thus taught, applied, and confirmed to us by this sacrament?*

Answer: As by baptism we were taught and assured that through the merit of Christ's passion, and of it only, we were first received into God's covenant and favor, united to Him and His church, and so obtained remission of all our sins and the grace of regeneration, so by this sacrament we are taught and assured that through the merit of Christ's passion, and of it only, we are and shall be kept in this blessed estate, nourished and confirmed in it, [and] revived and comforted in all temptations.

Question 25: *Declare this more particularly and fully, and first tell me why it was necessary that we should have not only a sacrament of our first entrance into God's favor and of our regeneration but also another sacrament of our nourishment and perseverance in the state of grace.*

Answer:

1. Though the graces confirmed by baptism can never totally be lost,[a] yet through our natural corruption and daily temptations the assurance, strength, and feeling of them will decay unless they be nourished.[b]

2. The only thing that causes us to persevere in faith and obedience, and gives us strength and comfort against all temptations,[c] is the remembrance and faith we have in the merit of Christ's passion, whereby He makes continual intercession unto His Father for us.[d] It was needful we should be taught and assured of this by this sacrament.

[a] 1 Peter 1:23; 1 John 3:9
[b] Ps. 51:10–12; 1 Thess. 5:19; Rev. 3:2
[c] Gal. 6:14; 1 John 5:4
[d] Heb. 7:25; 12:24

Question 26: *What means and helps have we in this sacrament to teach, apply, and confirm to us this promise of grace in so comfortable a manner as you have said?*

Answer:

1. Christ and His passion, and this nourishment and grace of perseverance that we receive by the merit thereof, are most clearly and sensibly represented to us in this sacrament.

2. Christ, and this benefit and merit of His passion, is more particularly offered and applied to us in this sacrament than in any other means.

3. Christ, and this benefit of His passion, is by this sacrament exhibited, given, and confirmed to us most fully and effectually.

4. The communion that we have with the true church of Christ, and the mutual love that should be in all Christians one toward another, is more clearly and fully represented and confirmed to us by this sacrament than by any other means.

Question 27: *How may Christ be said to be so clearly and sensibly[5] represented to us in this sacrament?*

Answer:

1. This is one end that this sacrament was ordained for, to put us in remembrance of Christ.[a]

2. By earthly creatures[6] and outward actions ordained by God, whereof all our senses can judge and discern, and by that fit and near proportion that is between them and that which is represented by them, the Lord does in this sacrament teach Christ unto us by all our senses, and consequently more plainly and familiarly than by the Word alone.[b]

[a] Luke 22:19; 1 Cor. 11:24–25
[b] See how profitable and necessary such sensible and visible instructions (ordained of God) have ever been esteemed: Gen. 9:13; Isa. 7:11; Jer. 19:10–11; Acts 12:11; John 3:12; Rom. 4:11

---

5. *Sensibly*: to our senses.
6. *Earthly creatures*: bread and wine.

Question 28: *But why did you say that in this sacrament the passion of Christ is so clearly and sensibly represented unto us?*

Answer: Because Christ in this sacrament is represented unto us in no other estate than that He was in when He was crucified;[a] and as the apostle [Paul] says that so oft as we celebrate this sacrament, we show forth the Lord's death till He come.[b]

[a] Matt. 26:28; 1 Cor. 11:24–25
[b] 1 Cor. 11:26

Question 29: *What helps have we here to represent and put us in mind of the passion of Christ?*

Answer: We have in this sacrament not only bread, which signifies His body, but wine, which signifies His blood. Whereby it is evident that Christ is here represented, offered, and given unto us as He was at that time when His blood was separated from His body.

Question 30: *But if the bread were dipped in the wine (as in some ancient churches it was wont to be, and is yet used[7] to be in some places), were it not every whit as sufficient to represent Christ unto us as if they were given and received severally[8] and apart?*

Answer: No, verily. For

1. Our faith in this sacrament is specially directed to the passion of Christ, as we have already shown.[a]

2. The death of Christ was not natural but violent and bloody,[b] and in His passion His blood was separated from His body and poured out and shed abundantly.[c]

3. It was necessary for our salvation that Christ should not only die but in His passion shed His blood for us, and so

---

7. *Used*: accustomed.
8. *Severally*: separately.

show Himself that only true means of the redemption of His church, which was shadowed and figured in all the sacrifices under the law.[d]

[a] 1 Cor. 11:26
[b] Acts 20:28; Eph. 1:7; Heb. 13:20; 1 Peter 1:19
[c] Luke 22:44; Ps. 22:16; John 20:25; 19:34
[d] Ex. 12:22; Heb. 11:28; Lev. 16:14–15; Num. 19:3, 5; Heb. 9:21

Question 31: *What other help have we in this sacrament to represent and put us in mind of the passion of Christ?*

Answer: The bread is solemnly in the sight of the congregation broken in sunder, and the wine poured forth, and that by the ordinance and commandment of Christ.

Question 32: *May not then whole cakes (as among the papists) be delivered and received in this sacrament?*[9]

Answer: No, verily.

Question 33: *How may that be proved?*

Answer:

1. Because in all those places of Holy Scripture where mention is made of this sacrament, this rite of the breaking of the bread is named.[a] Yea, the whole action in this sacrament is called breaking of bread,[b] and

---

9. "Bread or wafers (cakes)" became a controversial issue in Elizabethan England. Most Protestants saw wafers as a reversion to popery and wanted ordinary bread to be used. Despite the 1559 Book of Common Prayer ordering that bread should be used, the royal injunctions prescribed wafers. At a parish level, traditionalists refused bread when offered, and Protestants refused wafers. Bread finally won the day by the time of the 1604 Canons. For more details, see Christopher Haigh, "'A Matter of Much Contention in the Realm': Parish Controversies over Communion Bread in Post-Reformation England," *History* (July 2003): 393–404.

the apostle [Paul], repeating the words of institution, mentions this rite twice.[c]

2. Because the inward action that is represented to us thereby is most necessary for us to be put in mind of.

[a] Matt. 26:26; Mark 14:22; Luke 22:19
[b] Acts 2:42; 20:7
[c] 1 Cor. 11:26

Question 34: *What is that?*

Answer: The breaking of the body of Christ and shedding of His blood, yea, all those infinite torments that He did endure both in body and soul for us.[a]

[a] Isa. 53:5–6

Question 35: *As you have shown how Christ and His bloody passion is represented to us in this sacrament, so tell me what helps we have here to represent to our souls the nourishment and strength to persevere in the state of grace, which we receive by the merit of His passion.*

Answer: First, there is not one element only given and received here, but two, to teach that both meat and drink, which is sufficient nourishment for our souls, is to be found in Christ.[a]

[a] John 6:54–55, 35

Question 36: *But if bread alone were given to God's people in this sacrament (as in the Church of Rome), were not that sufficient, seeing the blood of Christ, as of all other living men, was and is contained in His body?*

Answer: No, verily. That cannot be done without manifest sacrilege, for

1. Christ in the institution of this sacrament ordained[a] and commanded all His disciples (and in them the whole

church which was, as I have before said, represented by them) that they should as well take and drink of the cup as eat the bread.[b] And the apostle [Paul], by virtue of this ordinance and institution, enjoined to all the Corinthians the use of the cup as well as of the bread.[c] Yea, the Lord (as foreseeing this sacrilege of the papists) has more expressly commanded the use of the cup to all than He has done the use of the bread.[d]

2. It was necessary that we should in this sacrament have two elements that might represent the full and sufficient nourishment and refection that we have in Christ. For else our state had been worse than of the people of God under the law, and our sacraments less clear than theirs.[e]

3. In that state wherein Christ is represented and offered to us in this sacrament (namely, in His passion), His blood was separated from His body.[f]

[a] Matt. 26:28; Mark 14:23; Luke 22:20
[b] Matt. 26:26–27; 1 Cor. 11:25
[c] 1 Cor. 11:26, 29
[d] Matt. 26:27–28; Mark 14:23–24
[e] 1 Cor. 10:3–4
[f] Luke 22:44; John 19:34

Question 37: *What other helps have we in this sacrament to represent to our souls the nourishment and strength to persevere in the state of grace, which we receive by the merit of Christ's passion?*

Answer:

1. *Bread* and *wine* are given and received here, which are most generally used throughout the world;[a] the one for the strengthening and nourishment of the body, the other for the quenching of the thirst, refreshing those that faint, and cheering the heart of those that are in heaviness.[b] Therefore they are most fit to represent

to the soul the strength[c] and refreshing[d] it receives by Christ.

2. This bread and wine is not only received in this sacrament, but every communicant does eat and drink it, and that by the commandment of Christ.[e] Which action, as it is of all other the chief means of nourishment and makes our food of the same substance with us, so is it most fit to represent the sound nourishment and comfort that we have by Christ and that we are by faith made all one with Him.[f]

[a] Ps. 104:14–15; Gen. 39:6; Matt. 6:11
[b] Pss. 104:15; 4:7; Prov. 31:6–7; 1 Tim. 5:23
[c] John 6:35
[d] Prov. 9:2, 5; Song 1:2, 4; 5:1; 7:9; John 15:1; Matt. 11:28
[e] Matt. 26:26–27; Mark 14:22–23; 1 Cor. 11:24
[f] John 6:35, 40, 51, 56; Eph. 5:30

Question 38: *As you have shown how Christ and His passion, and this benefit we receive by the merit thereof, is represented unto us, so tell me now how all this is more particularly offered and applied unto us in this sacrament than by any other means.*

Answer: The bread and wine is particularly offered, and every communicant (according to the commandment that is given in the name of Christ) does receive, eat, and drink the same.[a] This is most effectual to teach and persuade us that the Lord does offer and give us the body and blood of His Son,[b] and that (as it is the will of God that every one of us should[c]) everyone that comes worthily to this sacrament does indeed receive and apply Christ to himself for the nourishment and comfort of his soul.

[a] Matt. 26:26–27; Mark 14:22–23; Luke 22:17, 19; 1 Cor. 11:24–25
[b] John 6:32; Rom. 8:32
[c] 1 John 3:23

Question 39: *Why was it said that Christ and this benefit of His passion is not only represented and offered but verily exhibited and given unto us in this sacrament?*

Answer: Because this sacrament is not ordained to be a bare and naked sign, or as a picture that puts us in mind of one that is absent,[a] but to be a seal also, with and by which the Lord does verily convey and bestow Christ upon us and confirm and make sure to us this benefit of His passion, as lands are passed and conveyed among men by the sealing and delivery of deeds and indentures.[10]

[a] Rom. 4:11; 1 Cor. 10:16

Question 40: *Is Christ then indeed present with this sacrament?*[11]

Answer: Yes, verily. Christ Himself is not only signified and represented but truly present, given, and received in this sacrament. Yet He is present to the believer, not to the bread and wine; not corporally, but spiritually and sacramentally present.[a] He is not offered by the minister unto the body but by the Lord to the faith of the worthy receiver.

[a] John 6:63

Question 41: *How may it appear that Christ is not corporally present in this sacrament?*

Answer:

1. Because the sacraments that God's people enjoyed under the law were in substance the same with our sacraments, and in them Christ was not corporally present but only spiritually and sacramentally.[a]

---

10. This last phrase does not appear in the 1609 edition.

11. The 1609 edition has *in* rather than *with*. The answer is clarified and made more explicit in this later edition by adding the words *bread and wine* in the second line.

2. We receive no other thing, nor in any other manner, in the sacrament than the disciples did in the first institution thereof; and we are sure that Christ's body and blood were not corporally received by them but only spiritually and sacramentally.

3. As our Savior did oft foretell His disciples that (in respect of His bodily presence) He should leave the world and go unto His Father,[b] so He was indeed in the sight of them all taken up into heaven.[c] And God (who cannot lie) has told us that the heavens must contain Him until the end of the world.[d] So that if any shall say to us now, since the time of His ascension, here is Christ, or there He is, we are strictly charged not to believe it.[e]

4. We are sure that Christ has but one body and that His body even since His resurrection is a true body[f] and such as cannot be in many places at once.[g] And that it fills a place wheresoever it is, and may be both seen and felt.[h] Therefore it is not possible that He should be corporally present wheresoever this sacrament is administered, nor corporally received by everyone that receives this sacrament. And if it be impossible that His glorified body should be in many places at once, or in any place where it can neither be seen or felt, then much less can His crucified body (whereunto yet our faith is directed in this sacrament, and not unto His glorified body) be so.

5. Even if it were possible that He should be corporally present or corporally received in the sacrament, yet were it no way needful or profitable for us that it should be so. For as all the benefits that the church receives by Christ have been far more plentifully communicated unto her since His ascension into heaven than when He was corporally present with her upon earth (in which respect it was profitable for her to lose His bodily presence),[i] so the spiritual presence of Christ and our feeding on Him by faith is far more effectual to the comfort and salvation

of our souls than any bodily presence and feeding could possibly be.[j]

[a] 1 Cor. 10:3–4
[b] John 13:1; 14:2, 19, 25, 28; 16:4, 5, 7, 16, 28
[c] Luke 24:51; Acts 1:9–11
[d] Acts 3:21
[e] Matt. 24:23
[f] Heb. 10:5
[g] Matt. 28:6–7; Mark 16:6–7
[h] Mark 16:7; Luke 24:39; John 20:20, 27
[i] John 7:36; 16:7; 20:17
[j] John 6:62–63

Question 42: *Why, then, is the bread called the body of Christ, and the wine the blood of Christ?*

Answer:

1. The Lord has ever been wont in speaking of His sacraments to give unto the outward sign the name of the thing signified thereby.[a]

2. The reason why the Lord so speaks of sacraments is to show how certain and near that spiritual presence and union is, that by the power of His Spirit is made between the sign and the thing signified (howsoever far they be distant in place, the one from the other). And that as verily as the one is offered and given to the body, so certainly is the other offered and given to the soul of the faithful receiver.

3. This manner of speech is more plain and effectual to lift up our hearts from the earthly elements unto the consideration of the heavenly matter represented by them than if He should have called them only the signs of His body and blood.

[a] Gen. 17:10–11; Ex. 12:11; 24:8; 1 Cor. 10:4

Question 43: *You have shown me how Christ and His passion, and the benefit we receive thereby, is not only sensibly represented but particularly offered and applied, and verily exhibited also unto us. Now tell me how that communion which we have with all the faithful, and the mutual love that should be in all Christians one toward another, is represented and confirmed to us in this sacrament.*

Answer:

1. We are partakers of no other elements here than all the rest (not only of the same congregation where we receive without respect of persons) but of all the faithful throughout the world are partakers of.[a] This was one cause why our Savior made choice of bread and wine, which of all other creatures are most universally used throughout the world for the nourishment and comfort of the body.

2. This sacrament by the ordinance of Christ is to be administered in the most public congregation, and the sacramental actions to be performed by the minister (as near as conveniently they may be) but once for all that receive together.[b]

[a] 1 Cor. 10:17
[b] Matt. 26:26; Mark 14:22; Luke 22:19; 1 Cor. 11:24

Question 44: *How may it appear that the Lord has ordained that this sacrament should be administered publicly and not in private?*

Answer:

1. It has been the practice of God's church, commended in the Word, to celebrate the sacraments in solemn assemblies.[a]

2. The Lord has commanded His sacraments should be so celebrated,[b] and not otherwise.[c]

3. The sacraments are seals of the covenant of grace,[d] which is not appropriated to any few but is offered in common

to the whole church,[e] and wherein all (howsoever far they differ one from another in worldly respects) have equal interest. Therefore, as they do concern the public privileges of all, they must needs be actions of a public nature and should be publicly administered.

4. In the use of the sacraments, we make profession of our faith[f] and celebrate with praise and thanksgiving the remembrance of the great benefit of our redemption.[g] Both these duties are then performed in [a] most acceptable manner unto God when they are done in the most public and solemn assemblies of His people.[h]

5. The dignity and reverence due to the sacraments requires that they should be administered publicly in the assembly of all God's people and with the prayers of all.[i]

6. It may appear that in this sacrament the Lord requires this solemnity more than in any other He has given at any time to His church,

   i. because in it He has instituted such elements as might be common to the whole church,

   ii. and broke the bread and poured forth the wine but once in the sight of all,[j]

   iii. and spoke the words of institution but once to them all together,

   iv. and ordained it to this end (among others) to testify and confirm the mutual love that should be in all the faithful one toward another.

[a] Gen. 17:26–27; Luke 1:59; 2 Chron. 30:3, 5, 13; 35:18; Matt. 3:5, 6, 13; Luke 3:21; Acts 2:42; 20:7; 1 Cor. 11:18, 20
[b] Ex. 12:6, 47; Deut. 12:5, 9; Lev. 17:3, 4
[c] 1 Cor. 11:22, 33, 34
[d] Rom. 4:11
[e] Prov. 8:23; 9:3; Mark 16:15; Acts 2:39; 1 John 2:2; Matt. 26:28
[f] 1 Cor. 12:13; Gal. 3:27–28; Eph. 4:5; Jude 3
[g] Gen. 17:11; Ex. 13:9

^h Ex. 12:14; 1 Cor. 11:26
ⁱ Pss. 22:22; 40:9–10; 149:1
^j 2 Sam. 6:1, 2, 15

Question 45: *Do you then condemn all such as, being unable to come to the congregation, do desire this sacrament to be administered to them in private?*

Answer: No, but

1. All Christians are to be taught that they may not put off the receiving of this sacrament until their sickness, but receive it when they may with the rest of God's people in the public congregation, and that it is their ignorance and infirmity to desire it in private.

2. If at any time (upon extraordinary occasion) the sacrament be administered in a private house, yet ought a sufficient company of the faithful to be present and to communicate in it, and that not without the ministry and preaching of the Word.

Question 46: *How are Christians to be dissuaded from the desire of the sacraments in private?*

Answer:

1. By the consideration of what I have already said, to prove that it is the will of God that the sacrament should be administered in the public assemblies.

2. Because as they shall swerve therein from the example of the best instructed and Reformed churches and Christians, so they shall fashion themselves to such as are ignorant, popish, and profane, with whom these private communions ever have been and still are most in use.

3. Because they shall not hereby deprive themselves of the comfort and benefit of the sacrament in their sickness or in the hour of their death if they do not receive

it at that time. For the efficacy and fruit of this sacrament, which they received so often as they might[12] in the public congregation when they were in health, is not to be restrained[13] to the time of receiving but extends itself to the whole time of their life afterward.

4. Because it is folly and superstition to give that honor, or ascribe that necessity, to the sacrament as to think it can do us good being received or used otherwise than according to God's ordinance.[a] Whereas on the other side, we are to assure ourselves that the Lord both can and will help and comfort us without the outward means when we cannot have them in such sort as He has ordained but are deprived of them, not by our own negligence but by the hand of God.[b]

[a] 1 Sam. 4:3, 10; 2 Sam. 15:25
[b] Ezek. 11:16; Ps. 141:2

Question 47: *As you have shown at large how our communion with Christ and His church is both represented and confirmed to us by the bread and wine, the breaking and pouring forth, the giving and receiving of the same in this sacrament, so tell me now whether all bread and wine that is broken and poured forth, given and received, may not as well serve to represent and confirm these things unto us as these elements and actions that are used in this sacrament.*

Answer: No. For the bread and wine by nature serve only for the nourishment and comfort of the body; neither are they at all effectual to yield this strength or comfort to the soul, being used anywhere else but only in this sacrament.

---

12. The phrase *so often as they might* does not appear in the 1609 edition.
13. *Restrained*: restricted, confined.

Question 48: *How are these elements and actions in the sacrament made more effectual to represent and confirm these spiritual and heavenly things than the same elements and actions used anywhere else?*

Answer: By being consecrated and put apart from that use they served to by nature, unto this holy and spiritual use.

Question 49: *How are the elements and actions in this sacrament thus consecrated and put apart from that use they served to by nature, unto this holy and spiritual use?*

Answer: Partly by that which Christ Himself did in the first institution of this sacrament, and partly by that which the minister of the Word of God and the congregation do, whensoever this sacrament is administered according to the institution of Christ.[a]

[a] Matt. 26:26; Mark 14:22; 1 Cor. 10:16

Question 50: *How did Christ Himself consecrate these elements and actions unto this holy and spiritual use?*

Answer:

1. By the thanksgiving and prayer He made unto His Father at that time when He first instituted this sacrament.[a] Whereby it is said He blessed these elements—that is, obtained a special blessing from God upon them.[14]

2. By instituting and ordaining these elements and actions in this sacrament to serve unto this end; not only using them for Himself[b] but [by] commanding His church to do so also[c] and promising unto us His gracious and

---

14. This last sentence has been added for clarification but does not appear in the 1609 edition.

effectual presence in the use of these elements, according to His ordinance.[d]

[a] Matt. 26:26–27; Luke 22:19; 1 Cor. 11:24
[b] Matt. 26:26–27
[c] Luke 22:19; 1 Cor. 11:24–25
[d] "This is my body" (Matt. 26:26); "This is my blood" (Matt. 26:28)

Question 51: *How does the minister of the Word of God and the congregation consecrate these elements and sacramental actions?*

Answer:

1. By declaring the institution of this sacrament and how Christ did consecrate and put apart these elements and actions to this end and use, and [by] using them according to His institution.[a]

2. By giving public thanks unto God, both for the work of our redemption by the blood of His Son and also for making it known, offering [it], and assuring it unto us not only by His Word but most plainly and sensibly by this sacrament.[b]

3. By earnest prayer unto the Lord, that He would be present with and bless this His own ordinance, making it effectual to those ends that He Himself appointed it for.[c]

[a] 1 Tim. 4:4–5
[b] "according to Christ's example" (1 Tim. 4:4); Matt. 26:27; Mark 14:23; Luke 22:19; 1 Cor. 11:24
[c] 1 Tim. 4:5

Question 52: *But why do you mention the minister of Christ when you speak of the consecrating of this sacrament? Is it any matter who does consecrate it or deliver it, or at whose hands we do receive it?*

Answer: Yes, verily, for

1. As it is not lawful for any person without commission and authority from the king to use and apply the king's seal to convey any assurance in worldly matters, it is a heinous sin[15] for any, having no calling and commission thereunto from Christ, to take upon him to administer this sacrament, being the public seal of the King of kings and of the commonwealth of Israel.[a]

2. God has been wont severely to punish such as have taken upon them to deliver His sacraments without His calling and commission,[b] and has also been much offended with the people among whom this fault has been committed.[c]

> [a] "So when it was told John that Christ baptized, he answered none could do it without authority given him from heaven" (John 3:26–27); Rom. 4:11
> [b] 1 Chron. 13:10, 11; 15:12–13; 2 Chron. 26:16–20
> [c] 2 Chron. 13:9, 12, 15

Question 53: *How may this appear that only ministers and preachers of the Word of God have a calling and authority from Christ to administer this sacrament?*

Answer:

1. Because we find that all the sacraments which God has at any time instituted in His church have been committed by Him unto such as were ministers and preachers of the Word, that by them they might be delivered unto the church.[a] Insomuch as we read [that] the people of God could not celebrate the Passover until such time as the priests and Levites (who were appointed of God both

---

15. *Heinous sin:* 1609 edition has *great sin.*

to teach the people and to sacrifice, and minister the other sacraments) were sanctified and prepared unto that service.[b]

2. Only the ministers and preachers of the Word are, by reason of their special office and function, called in the Scriptures the Lord's stewards and disposers of His mysteries unto His church.[c]

3. They only are said to represent the Lord, and to bear His person, and to be in His stead unto us in the matters of His worship as the magistrate does in the civil government and affairs of this life.[d] So they are both His mouth unto us to deliver us His Word, and His hand unto us to deliver us His sacraments. And that which is done by them in these matters, according to His Word, is said to be done by the Lord Himself,[e] because He has promised to be present with them and to work with them, ratifying from heaven His own ordinance in their ministry.[f]

[a] Gen. 6:14; cf. 2 Peter 2:5; Gen. 17:23; cf. Gen. 20:7; Deut. 33:10; 2 Chron. 35:3, 6; Mark 1:4; Matt. 28:19
[b] 2 Chron. 30:3; 35:3–6; Ezra 6:19–20
[c] 1 Cor. 4:1–2
[d] 2 Cor. 5:20; Ex. 4:16
[e] John 4:1–2; Eph. 2:17; Luke 10:16
[f] Matt. 28:20

Question 54: *Does then the worthiness and efficacy of the sacrament depend upon the goodness of the minister that delivers it unto us?*

Answer: No. But it depends wholly upon the ordinance of God and upon the truth and power of Christ that did institute it. Yet must it needs make much for the security and comfort of a Christian to receive it from such a one as he knows has authority and commission from Christ to deliver it unto him.

Question 55: *As you have shown the necessity of a minister and preacher of the Word in the administration of this sacrament, so tell me whether it be needful that the Word should be always preached at the same time when this sacrament is to be administered.*

Answer: Yes, verily. For though to them that have already believed through the preaching of the gospel it may be a true sacrament and seal of God's covenant, though the Word be not preached immediately before being administered by a true minister of God, yet is the ordinance of God in some degree transgressed, and the comfort that God's people should receive by this sacrament greatly hindered, if at any time the sacrament be administered and that duty neglected.

Question 56: *How may that be proved?*

Answer:

1. Because we find that it has always been the practice of God's church, commended to us in the Holy Scriptures, to have the Word preached at all times when they have been assembled to receive the sacraments of the New Testament.[a]

2. Seeing the sacrament can never do us good until we have attained unto a true faith, which ordinarily is wrought by preaching, it must needs be most fit and profitable that whensoever the people of God are to receive this seal of the covenant of grace, they may have the covenant itself (whereupon the force and efficacy of the seal depends) published, opened, and applied unto them, considering the great need we all stand in (at that time especially) to have our faith quickened and stirred up in us and that no means can be so effectual to quicken it as that whereby it was first begotten.

[a] Mark 1:4; Acts 19:4; 10:34, 37, 47; 8:12, 35, 37, 38; 16:14, 15, 32, 33; 2:41, 42; 20:7

Question 57: *After that the bread and wine have been thus consecrated by the minister of Christ, are they not then by virtue of this consecration changed from that which they were before?*

Answer: Yes, but they are changed only in their use, not in their nature, because here they are not used to that end that other bread and wine are used for—namely, to the nourishment and comfort of the body—but to a holy and spiritual end. But the substance of the bread and wine remain the very same after the consecration that it was before.

Question 58: *How may that be proved?*

Answer:

1. Because the Scripture calls them bread and wine even after they were consecrated.[a]

2. It can be no sacrament unless such an outward sign remain as is by good proportion fit to represent the nourishment and refreshing we have by Christ, which the substance only of the bread and wine (and not of the accidents thereof) is able to do.

3. If the substance of the bread and wine were changed into the body and blood of Christ, it were not possible that by long keeping they should putrefy and corrupt.[b]

4. If the substance of the bread and wine were changed into the very body and blood of Christ, then the reprobate who receive this sacrament should also eat the flesh and drink the blood of Christ, which is impossible and contrary to the Holy Scriptures.[c]

[a] 1 Cor. 10:16; 11:27, 28
[b] Acts 2:31
[c] John 6:54, 56; 1:12

Question 59: *If any of that bread and wine (that stood on the Lord's Table when the elements and the whole action was in this sort consecrated, as you have said) do remain after the administration of the sacrament is ended, does it then differ from common bread and wine, or is it more holy by virtue of this consecration?*

Answer: No, verily. For seeing the consecration, as we have heard, changes them not in nature but in use only, and one part of the consecration stands in using them according to Christ's institution; no more of the bread and wine can be holy than is given and received in this sacrament.

Question 60: *As you have shown at large that none can receive this sacrament worthily but [only] such as find in themselves an unfeigned and earnest desire to it, and declared also the reasons that should move us to desire it, so tell me now what use is to be made of all this doctrine.*

Answer: It serves principally for reproof of two sorts of people:

1. Of them that, not being withheld by sickness or like necessary impediments, do, either out of too base an estimation they have of this sacrament or out of a careless neglect to prepare themselves unto it, absent themselves from it when it is administered in the congregation whereof they are members.

2. Of such as receive it sometimes yet without a sincere and right desire of it or any appetite unto it at all, but [receive it] either for that they would thereby escape the danger of laws, or because they would conform themselves to the custom of the place where they live, or upon a superstitious persuasion that it will purge them from all their sins and infuse grace and holiness into their souls.

Question 61: *Is every Christian then bound to receive this sacrament every time that it is administered in that congregation whereof he is a* *member, unless he be by sickness or some such likely impediment kept from it?*

Answer: Yes, surely. For it is [as] necessary to receive this sacrament when we may as it is to hear the Word preached when we may[a] and as it is for them that are converted to the faith and for Christian parents (the one for themselves, the other for their children) to seek and desire the sacrament of baptism upon the first opportunity that God shall offer unto them.[b]

[a] 1 Thess. 5:19–20; Heb. 2:3
[b] Acts 2:41; 8:12, 36; 16:33; 22:16

Question 62: *How may it appear to be a sin of such danger to neglect thus the receiving of this sacrament?*

Answer:

1. The zeal and desire that God's people under the law showed unto their sacraments, and the pains and cost they were at to enjoy them, being by the Holy Ghost commended to us in the Word for our imitation, should make us ashamed of our coldness and careless neglect of this sacrament,[a] which in respect both of the clearness of it[b] and of the person that did first institute it[c] is far more great and excellent than they were.

2. The great severity of God in threatening and punishing the neglect of His sacraments under the law is recorded in the Scriptures to admonish us, and may assure us that He will much less bear with the neglect of this sacrament.[d]

3. This neglect of coming to this sacrament when we may argues our shameful unthankfulness for the great benefit of our redemption by the death of Christ, which in this sacrament (that has been therefore called the *Eucharist*) we are appointed to celebrate the remembrance of with solemn praise and thanksgiving.[e]

4. It argues a profane and open contempt both of the commandment of our Savior Christ, who has charged us to come—and to come often—to this sacrament, and of those inestimable benefits which He offers us in it, and of the church and people of God, from whose fellowship we do thus divide and excommunicate ourselves.[f] Which sin we may be well assured the Lord must needs be highly offended with.[g]

[a] Num. 9:7; 2 Chron. 30:1, 5, 21, 26; 35:7, 18; Luke 2:41
[b] Mark 11:11
[c] Heb. 3:5–6; cf. Heb. 11:28
[d] Gen. 17:14; Ex. 4:24–26; Num. 9:13
[e] 1 Cor. 11:26
[f] 1 Cor. 11:24–26
[g] Isa. 7:12–13; Matt. 22:7; Luke 14:24; Heb. 2:3

Question 63: *But if a man find himself through uncharitableness or worldly distractions unfit and unprepared, is it not then much better for him to abstain than to come to this sacrament?*

Answer: Indeed, no man ought to come that finds himself unprepared. But this is no excuse for them that do not so much the more carefully endeavor to prepare themselves. For

1. They that choose rather to deprive themselves of the benefit of this sacrament than they will freely forgive such as have wronged them, or seek reconciliation, or take pains to prepare their hearts unto it, do show manifest contempt of God's mercy and judge themselves unworthy of Christ and all His merits, and shall one day be judged despisers of their own salvation.[a]

2. While by uncharitableness and carelessness to prepare themselves they refuse this sacrament, they can have no hope that either the Word[b] or prayer[c] should do them good. And therefore by this reason, they may as well abstain from hearing or reading the Word and praying as from this sacrament.

3. They that feel that they are not only void of malice them-selves but also unfeignedly willing to use all means of reconciliation with such as do malice them ought not to suffer the hatred of others to keep them from this sacrament.[d] But rather, the more they are injured by men, the more need they have to seek comfort in the Lord by this His holy ordinance.[e]

[a] Acts 13:46
[b] James 1:20–21; 1 Peter 2:1–2
[c] Mark 11:25–26
[d] 2 Cor. 8:12
[e] 1 Sam. 30:6

Question 64: *As you have shown the sin of those that willingly absent themselves from this sacrament when they may receive it, so tell me how they may also appear to be in great fault that use[16] to receive it but yet either without any desire and appetite unto it or without a sincere and right desire.*

Answer:

1. Because as in all the service we do to God it is required that we do it not grudgingly or as of necessity but with cheerfulness and fervency of spirit.[a] So is it especially required that we come to this heavenly banquet with appetite and delight because of the great benefits that we celebrate the remembrance of and that are offered and confirmed to us in it.[b]

2. If our desire do arise from any other ground than from the consideration of those reasons we have already mentioned (as first, either from the commandment of our superiors, or second, the desire we have to be neighbor-like, or third, from this conceit that the deed done will purge us from our sins), we do not serve the Lord in coming to this sacrament but men and our own

---

16. *Use*: are accustomed.

selves.[c] And so [we] make ourselves guilty of a heinous profanation of this sacrament.

[a] Deut. 28:47; 1 Chron. 28:9; Ps. 2:11; 2 Cor. 8:12; 9:7; Acts 2:41; Rom. 12:11
[b] Deut. 12:7; 16:15; 1 Sam. 1:7
[c] Zech. 7:5–6; Rom. 14:6–20

Question 65: *May not, then, magistrates and other superiors command and compel such as live under their government to receive this sacrament if they shall discern them to be careless of it?*

Answer: Everyone that is in authority may and must also use all means to persuade all such as are under him to [have] a desire of this sacrament,[a] and command and compel them also to receive it.[b] Yea, he must judge them unworthy to live in any Christian family or commonwealth that will not receive it.[c] But he may not compel any to receive whom he knows to be altogether uninstructed and unwilling, because (besides the profanation of the Lord's holy ordinance that is caused thereby) the man that receives unwillingly shall undoubtedly receive his own condemnation.

[a] Ex. 12:26–27; 2 Chron. 17:7
[b] Gen. 18:19; 2 Kings 23:21; 2 Chron. 14:4; 33:16; 34:33
[c] 2 Chron. 15:13

Question 66: *Hitherto you have declared how all that would come worthily to this sacrament must find in themselves a sincere and right desire unto it, which (as you have said) is the first grace required in our preparation thereunto. Tell me now, what is that knowledge which you mentioned as the second grace that every man must find in himself that would come worthily to this sacrament?*

Answer:

1. Everyone must have that measure of knowledge in the law of God (the sum whereof is contained in the Ten Commandments) as may serve to discover unto him not

only in general the corruption of his nature, whereby he is quite fallen from that holiness and righteousness that God requires of him and become prone to all evil, but also some special and particular sins he has committed, and the intolerable curse of God due to him for the same.[a]

2. Everyone must have that measure of knowledge in the gospel as may serve to make known unto him and certainly to assure him of the sufficiency both of that remedy that is to be found in Christ against all his sins and the curse of God and also of the means whereby that remedy is to be made his own—namely, a lively faith.[b]

3. Everyone must have that measure of knowledge in the doctrine of the sacrament as may serve to make known to him those helps that God has ordained in it, both for the representing and making known of Christ and His merits to all that receive it and also for the applying and confirming of them unto himself.[c]

[a] Jer. 3:13; Matt. 9:12; Rom. 3:20
[b] John 17:3; Matt. 16:18; 1 Cor. 2:12; Rev. 3:18
[c] Ex. 12:26–27; 13:8, 14

Question 67: *How may it appear that this measure of knowledge is necessarily required of all that come worthily to this sacrament?*

Answer:

1. Because knowledge is the foundation and beginning of all saving graces.[a] Neither can any man receive any comfort by Christ or any of His ordinances unless he be first enlightened with the knowledge of the truth.

2. Because until a man by the knowledge of the law have his sin (and the curse of God due to him for sin) effectually discovered to him,[b] and by the knowledge of the gospel the sufficiency of that remedy that is to be found

in Christ against all his sins and the curse of God,[c] he can never desire nor esteem of Christ. And until a man by the knowledge of this sacrament can discern the helps he may have in it for the quickening and increase of his faith, he can never desire it nor come with appetite unto it.

3. Seeing none can receive worthily but he that is able to examine himself,[d] and the only rule whereby a man is to examine himself is the Word of God, which consists of these two parts, the law and the gospel,[e] it must needs follow that he who wants[17] that competency of knowledge that I have spoken of cannot choose but be an unworthy receiver of the Lord's Supper if he presume to come to it.

[a] Prov. 19:2; 1 Tim. 2:4; Acts 26:18
[b] Rom. 3:20; Matt. 9:12; Gal. 3:24
[c] John 4:10
[d] 1 Cor. 11:28–29
[e] James 1:23–24; 2:12; John 12:48

Question 68: *What use is to be made of this doctrine concerning the necessity of knowledge in them that desire to come to the Lord's Table?*

Answer:

1. To teach us that before the Communion be administered to any people or they be urged to receive it, there should be care had that they be first catechized and instructed,[a] as we never read that either John the Baptist or any of the apostles did minister the sacraments to any people whom they had not first preached unto and instructed.

2. To discover the sin and fearful estate of the greatest part of communicants in this land, who though they be utterly ignorant in the principles of religion, and want

---

17. *Wants*: lacks.

the means of knowledge, and be void of all love and desire of knowledge or the means thereof, yet will [they] by no means be kept from receiving this sacrament, at Easter especially.[b] Which one sin, in so general a profanation of this sacrament, were sufficient to bring upon the land all those grievous judgments that have been and are still upon it, though it were guilty of no other sin besides.[c]

[a] Matt. 28:19
[b] Eccl. 1:17
[c] 1 Cor. 11:30–31

Question 69: *As you have shown the necessity of a desire to this sacrament, and of knowledge also in every one that would come worthily unto it, so tell me now what that faith is which you said was the third grace that is necessarily required to the preparing of us unto this sacrament.*

Answer: No man can receive this sacrament worthily unless he has a true justifying faith and be undoubtedly assured that Christ with all His merits do belong unto himself.

Question 70: *How may it appear that none can be worthy or fit to receive but that they have this faith?*

Answer:

1. Because this was necessarily required of all such as did desire to be baptized.[a]

2. This and all other [of] the sacraments are appointed of God, not to begin but to confirm faith where it is already begun,[b] and are therefore called seals of the righteousness that is by faith.[c]

3. As the Word of God that we hear cannot profit us at all unless it be mixed with faith, so much less can any profit by this visible word that wants faith,[d] which is both the

only eye, whereby we may discern the Lord's body,[e] and the hand and mouth, whereby we receive it and feed upon it.[f]

4. It is not possible that any should have that right desire to this sacrament, which we have already shown to be so necessary to our worthy receiving of it, that is not by a lively faith assured that Christ with all His merits do belong unto him.

[a] Mark 16:16; Acts 8:37; 16:31–34
[b] Rom. 10:14, 17
[c] Rom. 4:11
[d] Heb. 4:2
[e] John 3:14–15; 8:56
[f] John 1:12; 6:35–36; Eph. 3:17

Question 71: *But seeing it is evident by the Scriptures that Christ with His merits do not belong unto all men[a] but to a little flock,[b] and that the greatest part of the world,[c] and even of those that live in the profession of the true religion, shall receive no benefit by Him,[d] how can any poor sinner (that knows himself to be as unworthy to receive so great a gift from God as any other man) attain to this undoubted assurance that he is one of that little flock that Christ died for?*

Answer: The faith of God's elect is no vain fancy nor uncertain hope but a certain assurance, because it is grounded upon the Word of God,[e] which is infallible[f] and wrought in the heart by the Spirit of God,[g] which cannot lie.[h]

[a] John 17:9
[b] Luke 12:32
[c] Matt. 7:14
[d] Matt. 22:14
[e] Rom. 10:8
[f] Ps. 19:7–9
[g] Gal. 5:22; Rom. 8:16
[h] Titus 1:2; Heb. 6:18

Question 72: *But how is any particular man able to ground this assurance of his own salvation upon the Word of God? Or, what motives may a man find in the Word to persuade him undoubtedly that he shall be saved and that Christ with all His merits do belong unto him?*

Answer:

1. That Christ Jesus has by His death and obedience fully satisfied the justice of God and purchased eternal life for all that can believe in Him.[a]

2. That Christ with all His merits are by God's ordinance in the ministry of the Word[b] offered indefinitely[18] to everyone that hears the gospel, and especially to everyone that (out of the feeling of the burden and danger of his sins) can thirst after Him.[c]

3. That everyone that hears the gospel (especially everyone that feeling the burden and danger of his sin can thirst after Christ[d]) is strictly charged and commanded by the Lord in His Word to believe that Christ and all His merits do belong unto himself.[e]

4. That no sin or rebellion[f] that a man can possibly commit against God is accounted so heinous in His sight as infidelity,[19] when a man will not believe that Christ belongs to him, because in this he makes God a liar, as if offering His Son to him in His gospel and commanding him to believe, He should not mean as He speaks.[g]

[a] Isa. 53:5–6; 40:2; Matt. 17:5
[b] Mark 16:15; Acts 2:39
[c] Isa. 61:1–3; Matt. 9:12–13
[d] Matt. 11:28
[e] Mark 1:15; Matt. 22:9; Luke 14:21–23; Mark 11:24; cf. Matt. 6:12; 1 Peter 1:13; 1 John 3:23
[f] John 16:9; Matt. 16:16
[g] 1 John 5:10

---

18. *Indefinitely*: indiscriminately, freely.
19. *Infidelity*: unbelief.

Question 73: *What use is to be made of this doctrine touching the necessity of a lively faith for the receiving of this sacrament worthily?*

Answer:

1. To persuade everyone that professes himself to be a Christian to labor for a lively faith, which, as it is the root and foundation of all true comfort both in life and in death,[a] so without it, it is impossible that either this or any other service we do unto God (seem it otherwise never so good) should be acceptable unto Him or profitable to ourselves.[b]

2. To teach us that, because this faith is the mighty and supernatural work of God, and we are of ourselves by nature every whit as unable (if not more) to believe in Christ aright [as we are] to keep all God's commandments, it stands upon us to make high account of the ministry of the Word preached.[c] This is the means that God has chosen and appointed to show His mighty power in, for the begetting of faith in the hearts of His elect.[d] In the use of that holy ordinance of God [we should] cry earnestly unto Him for His blessing upon it.[e]

3. To discover[20] the fearful condition of them that living altogether without the ministry of the Word preached, and wanting[21] it willingly, or having never profited by it at all, do yet ordinarily receive this sacrament. Whereas no man (without an extraordinary and miraculous work of God, and such as He has never been wont to work when the ordinary means might be had[f]) can be worthy and fit to receive the Lord's Supper until he has first enjoyed the ministry of the Word and been an ordinary and fruitful hearer of the same.

[a] Jer. 9:24; Acts 16:34; Rom. 5:1–3; Luke 2:29–30
[b] Heb. 11:6; John 15:4; Acts 15:9; Titus 1:15

---

20. *Discover:* uncover, understand.
21. *Wanting:* lacking.

[c] Eph. 2:8; John 6:44; Eph. 1:19–20
[d] Rom. 1:16; 10:14; 1 Peter 1:23
[e] Ps. 119:33–36; Prov. 2:3–5
[f] Josh. 5:12

Question 74: *You have shown the necessity of the three first graces [a true desire, knowledge, and a lively faith], which you said were required to make a man worthy and fit to come unto the Lord's Table. Tell me now what that repentance is, without which, you said, no man can receive worthily.*

Answer: No man can come worthily unto this sacrament unless he has first unfeignedly repented—that is, both cast off all his known sins[a] (upon a hearty sorrow that he offended God by them,[b] and an unfeigned detestation he bears to them[c]) and also fully purposed and resolved with himself never to return to them again.[d]

[a] Prov. 28:13; Isa. 55:5–6; Jonah 3:10
[b] 2 Cor. 7:10
[c] Ezek. 18:31; Rom. 12:9
[d] 2 Cor. 11:7; Ps. 18: 23

Question 75: *How may it appear that none can be worthy or fit to come to the Lord's Table until he has thus repented?*

Answer:

1. Because we find that under the law none might be admitted to the Passover that had not separated themselves from the filthiness of the heathen[a] and cleansed themselves from all legal pollutions.[b]

2. Because the conscience defiled with any known sin corrupts all the holy things of God unto us.[c]

3. Because it is not possible that any man should have a true and lively faith, and assurance of the forgiveness of his sins, that has not thus unfeignedly repented.[d]

[a] Ezra 6:21

[b] Num. 9:6; 2 Chron. 23:19; 35:15; John 11:55
[c] Hag. 2:13–14; Titus 1:15; Heb. 10:22
[d] Mark 1:15; Matt. 21:32; Acts 3:26; 5:31

Question 76: *What use is to be made of this doctrine concerning the necessity of repentance?*

Answer: To persuade every man to labor and take pains with his own heart both to find out and know his special sins and to bring his heart to this unfeigned repentance for them, especially at that time when he prepares himself to come to the Lord's Table. Because as without this repentance it is not possible that we should come worthily unto it, so it will make whatsoever service we do unto God far more acceptable to Him and fruitful to ourselves when before such time as we draw near unto God therein we do first (out of that child-like fear and love we bear unto Him) cast away such sins as we know by ourselves.[a]

[a] James 4:8; Gen. 35:2–5; Judg. 10:16; 1 Sam. 7:3–4; Jonah 3:8–10

Question 77: *What principal points are there in God's Word by the meditation whereof our senseless and profane hearts may be moved unto this repentance?*

Answer: It will be profitable for us to consider of these points following:

1. That for the transgressing of God's commandment, even in a small thing, not only our first parents and all the race of mankind were deprived of eternal happiness and all grace to do well, and became subject to everlasting damnation in the life to come and infinite miseries in this life, and unto such a corruption of nature as whereby they are made prone to all manner of sin,[a] but also an infinite number of angels (the most excellent creatures that ever God made) did not only lose their happiness but became the most miserable and accursed creatures of all the rest.[b]

2. The fearful plagues that for sin God has brought upon sundry persons and parts of the world in old time,[c] and does still every day;[d] upon the whole world in the general flood;[e] upon the Jews, whom of all other people He once loved best;[f] and upon many of His most dear children.[g] All which are recorded in the Word and executed in our sight and hearing for us to consider and profit by.[h]

3. The unspeakable and infinite torments which the Son of God in His passion endured for us, as well in His soul as in His body,[i] without which we could never have been redeemed from the least of all our sins, nor from the intolerable wrath of God due to us for the same.[j]

[a] Rom. 5:14–19
[b] 2 Peter 2:4
[c] Rom. 1:18; 1 Cor. 10:5–15; 2 Peter 2:6
[d] Ps. 7:11; Zeph. 3:5; Eph. 5:6
[e] 2 Peter 2:5
[f] Rom. 11:21–22; 1 Thess. 2:16
[g] 2 Sam. 12:10–12; Ps. 51:8; Job 13:26
[h] 1 Cor. 10:11
[i] Zech. 12:10; Isa. 53: 3–5; Matt. 26:37–38; Luke 22:41–44; Matt. 27:46; Heb. 5:7
[j] 1 Peter 1:18–19; Gal. 3:13; 1 John 1:7

Question 78: *What mean you by that newness of life, which you said was the fifth grace that is required of them that would come worthily to this sacrament?*

Answer: No man can be fit to receive this sacrament that does not unfeignedly love the Lord and His holy Word and that is not only willing but able also in some measure to obey Him in all things, being fruitful in all good works, especially in the duties of his special calling.

Question 79: *How may it appear that there is such necessity of this newness of life that you have spoken of?*

Answer:

1. Because we find that under the law none might be admitted unto the Passover unless he were not only circumcised himself but did circumcise also all the males that did belong unto him.[a]

2. Because no man is within the covenant of grace (and consequently, this sacrament which is the seal thereof can belong to none) but such only as to whom God has given a new heart and a new spirit, and in whose hearts He has written His law and put His Spirit within them, to cause them to walk in His statutes and to keep His judgments and do them.[b]

3. Because no man can say he has a true faith (without which, as we have heard before, this sacrament can do us no good) unless he feels it working in him by love,[c] a consciousness of all God's holy commandments,[d] and not only a desire but some ability also and strength to do His will,[e] especially in the duties of his special calling.[f]

[a] Ex. 12:48
[b] Jer. 31:31; Ezek. 36:26–27
[c] Gal. 5:6
[d] Luke 1:6; Acts 24:16
[e] Matt. 3:10 [2 Cor. 5:17 included in 1609 edition]
[f] Ps. 1:3

Question 80: *What use is to be made of this doctrine concerning the necessity of newness of life in them that would come worthily to this sacrament?*

Answer: To show that the desire that most men have to this sacrament (as also their knowledge, faith, and repentance) is counterfeit and hypocritical, and consequently their coming to this sacrament [is] dangerous and damnable. Because that howsoever they profess these things, yet are they altogether void of the practice of piety and righteousness, and perform not any duty constantly and holily, either unto God in the exercises of His religion (public or private), or unto man in the particular duties of their calling, or in the general duties of justice and mercy.

Question 81: *What is that charity[22] which is the sixth and last of all those graces that you said were necessary for the preparing and making of us worthy to come to the Lord's Table?*

Answer: No man can be worthy and fit to come unto the Lord's Table that

1. Does not unfeignedly forgive all that have [in] any way offended him,[a] and cast off all purpose and desire of revenge.[b]

2. Is not willing (in love and obedience to God and desire to win his neighbor unto peace) to seek reconciliation with all such as he has been at variance with,[c] yea though they be[d] his inferiors,[23] and though the offense began on their part.[e]

3. Does not love all men[f] (even his enemies[g]), and that not in word only but in deed and truth, being ready by all means to do them good.[h]

4. Does not bear an entire and brotherly affection to all the godly,[i] abounding so much the more in love to them as he sees the graces of God to abound in them.[j]

[a] Col. 3:13; Matt. 18:35
[b] Rom. 12:19; 1 Thess. 5:15
[c] Pss. 34:14; 120:7; Matt. 5:23–24
[d] Gen. 13:8; 1 Peter 5:5

---

22. *Charity*: this was called *love* in the original list of six graces given in Answer 18. Here it also includes giving to those in need.

23. *Inferiors*: lower in social status.

[e] Matt. 18:15
[f] 1 Thess. 3:12
[g] Matt. 5:44
[h] 1 John 3:18; Eph. 4:32; Rom. 12:9
[i] Matt. 12:50; 1 John 3:14
[j] Ps. 16:3

Question 82: *How may it appear that this charity you speak of is so necessary as that without it none can receive this sacrament worthily?*

Answer:

1. Because it is often said in the Holy Scriptures that no service we do to God can be acceptable unto Him or profitable to ourselves while we be out of charity with our neighbors.[a]

2. Above all the parts of God's service, charity is principally required in the receiving of this sacrament. Because as we do herein make open profession of our union with Christ and with His church, so one principal end for which it was instituted was to confirm and increase our love one toward another.[b] Yea, whatsoever benefit is offered therein unto us we can no other way be capable of than as we are united and knit together as lively and feeling members to the whole body of God's church,[c] which also was the cause why our Savior in the institution of this sacrament, and administering it to His disciples, labored with them in nothing so much as to confirm them in love and charity one with another.[d]

3. It is not possible that any man should have true faith that wants charity,[e] or be assured that God has pardoned his sins that is not able to forgive them that have offended him.[f]

[a] Matt. 5:23–24; 1 Tim. 2:8; 1 Peter 3:7; 2:1–2; James 1:20
[b] 1 Cor. 10:16–17
[c] Eph. 3:6; 4:16
[d] John 13:14, 34, 35

^e 1 Cor. 13:2
^f Matt. 6:12, 14, 15; 18:35

Question 83: *What use is to be made of this doctrine concerning the necessity of charity in all them that desire this sacrament to their comfort?*

Answer: To persuade every Christian, as at all other times so especially then when he prepares himself to come to the Lord's Table, to strive against his uncharitableness and seriously to labor to bring his heart unto this love that has been described.

Question 84: *But seeing we are all by nature void of hearty love, even toward them that never wronged us, and marvelously prone to suspect, backbite, and malice all men (yea, we are unnatural, unkind, and unthankful even toward them to whom we are most nearly bound), tell me by what means we may be persuaded to forgive and bear this hearty love to them that are our enemies.*

Answer: It shall be profitable for us to consider of these things following:

1. That which we have to forgive the greatest enemy we can possibly have is nothing in comparison to that which we desire and hope the Lord will forgive us.^a And that the Lord will never remit to us that were His enemies the ten thousand talents we owe to Him if we be not able to remit to our brother the hundred pence that he owes us.^b And that if we did rightly believe and consider how merciful and kind the Lord has been unto us, and how much He has forgiven us, we could not choose but readily and cheerfully to forgive and love our greatest enemies^c because He will have us to do so.²⁴

---

24. *because He will have us to do so*: this phrase does not appear in the 1609 edition.

2. That the man whom we so hate is our fellow servant [and] professor of the same religion with us[d]—yea, our brother that has the Lord to his Father and the true church for his mother, as well as we, and is fellow heir with us of the grace of life.[e] And, admit[25] he be yet uncalled and a most wicked man, yet he is one whom we see the Lord our God vouchsafes[26] many favors unto, and whose conversion He seeks by all means,[f] whom He has so dearly and tenderly loved that He spared not His own Son but sent Him to endure infinite torments in soul and body even for him.[g] And that there is no grace in us, nor love unto God, if we cannot love them that we see are so dear unto Him.[h]

3. That our enemy is but the Lord's instrument.[i] And the wrongs he has done us are not permitted only, but sent from God, and that though our enemy has no just cause given him to deal so with us, yet the Lord has.[j] And therefore when we can discern the Lord's just hand in the wrongs [that] are done us, and receive that spiritual profit which God's children have always received by His corrections, we shall have no just cause to rage against him, whom the Lord uses as His instrument to humble and reform us by.[k]

4. That we ourselves have either wronged others as much as our enemy has done us, or at least we have been prone to do it.[l] And how can we so much abhor another for that fault which we ourselves are so subject unto?[m]

5. That the hurt we have received from our enemy, or that we can do to him by private revenge, is not comparable to that which we shall do to ourselves if we continue in malice. For besides that, we do thereby make God our enemy and cut ourselves from all hope that He should

---

25. *Admit*: even if.
26. *Vouchsafes*: graciously condescends to grant.

take our part and revenge our quarrel.[n] We do also deprive ourselves of all benefit by the Word and sacraments and prayer (as I have above shown). Yea, we cause them all to turn into poison unto us.

And what desperate folly were this in us, to kill ourselves that we might hurt our enemies?

[a] Matt. 18:24–28
[b] Matt. 6:15; 18:15
[c] Matt. 18:33; 1 John 4:11
[d] Gen. 50:17; Matt. 18:33; 24:49
[e] Gen. 13:8; Acts 7:26; Mal. 2:10; 1 Peter 3:7
[f] Matt. 5:45; Rom. 2:4
[g] John 3:16; 1 John 2:2
[h] 1 John 5:1
[i] Isa. 10:5; 45:7; Lam. 3:37; Job 1:21; 2 Sam. 16:10
[j] Pss. 39:9; 119:75
[k] 2 Sam. 16:10; Job 1:20–21
[l] Eccl. 7:23–24; Gal. 6:1
[m] 2 Chron. 28:10
[n] Prov. 24:17–18; 25:21–22; 20:22; Num. 12:3, 9, 10; 2 Sam. 16:12

Question 85: *Is it then the duty of a Christian to love and think well of all men?*

Answer: No, verily. For he may and ought

1. To hate the enemies of God[a]

2. To censure and judge the tree by his fruit, disliking and thinking evil of all such as by their deeds declare themselves to be wicked men[b]

Yea, he may not only

3. Shun all voluntary familiarity with them[c] but also

4. By countenance and other means witness his dislike and show himself strange unto them[d] so that he be privy[27] to himself in the uprightness of his heart

---

27. *Privy*: here this has the meaning of being true to himself.

    i. that he dislikes them for their sins against God, not for the wrongs they have done to himself;[e]

    ii. that he takes no pleasure to hear or speak of their sins[f] but can mourn for them;[g]

    iii. that he rejoices not in, nor desires, their hurt[h] but is able heartily to pray for them;[i]

    iv. [and is] both ready and desirous to show them kindness when he can see any cause to hope that he may do them good and win them unto God.[j]

[a] 2 Chron. 19:2; Ps. 139:21; Prov. 29:27
[b] Matt. 7:16–20; 1 Cor. 5:12; Prov. 17:15; Ps. 15:4
[c] Ps. 26:4–5; Rom. 16:17; 2 Thess. 3:14–15
[d] 2 Chron. 19:2; Prov. 25:23; 3 John 10; Job 8:20; Mark 3:5
[e] Pss. 69:9; 139:21
[f] 1 Cor. 13:6
[g] Ps. 119:136, 138, 139
[h] Prov. 17:5; 24:17–18; Job 31:29
[i] Ps. 35:13–14; Jer. 18:20
[j] Matt. 5:44; Gal. 6:10; 1 Thess. 4:12

Question 86: *In describing that charity which is required in all who would receive this sacrament to their comfort, you said we must unfeignedly forgive all that have [in] any way offended us, and cast off all purpose and desire of revenge. But tell me how far forth we are bound to forgive them that have wronged us, and whether it be utterly unlawful for us to seek our remedy against such as have done us injury in our person, or goods, or good name.*

Answer:

1. As it is unlawful for a Christian to be easily provoked unto wrath or dislike of his neighbor,[a] so after that he is justly provoked he must be easy to be appeased[b] and desirous of reconciliation,[c] willing to use all good means whereby to win him.[d] Yea, he is bound in whatsoever wrong he has received from any so to forgive it as he can love the party and think as well of him as he did before,[e]

as soon as he shall show himself sorrowful and penitent for the wrong he has done.

2. In [a] case [in which] the party that has wronged him will not be brought to see his fault and show himself penitent, though he may justly dislike him, yet may he not hate or recompense evil for evil unto him[f] but rather endure this or more injury at his hands than to do, or speak, or desire aught against him in private revenge.[g]

3. In [a] case [in which] the wrong has been such as whereby he is not only offended but hurt and damaged also in his person, or goods, or good name, it may be lawful for him to seek his remedy against him that has done the wrong, at the hands of the lawful magistrate. For as the magistracy and law are the ordinance of God,[h] so it may be lawful for a Christian (in the necessary defense or repair of his person, goods, or good name which God has bound every man to maintain and have a care of[i]) to take the benefit of it, provided that he observe those cautions and rules that God has given in His Word to direct us in this case.[j]

[a] Prov. 16:32; 19:11; 1 Cor. 13:4, 5, 7; Gal. 5:22–23
[b] James 3:17; Rom. 1:30
[c] Rom. 12:18
[d] Matt. 18:15; Luke 17:3
[e] Luke 17:3–4
[f] Matt. 5:43–44; Rom. 12:17
[g] Matt. 5:39; Job 31:30
[h] 2 Chron. 19:6; Rom. 13:1–4
[i] Eph. 5:29; 1 Tim. 5:22; Prov. 6:1; 10:4; 1 Tim. 5:8; Job 27:5–6; Prov. 22:1
[j] Ex. 22:1–15; Acts 16:37; 22:25; 23:17–24; 25:10–11

Question 87: *Which be those cautions and rules to be observed in going to law?*

Answer:

1. That we go not to law with any but in [the] case of necessity—that is, not for trifles[a] but only when the wrong is so great that if it be not righted by law we cannot conveniently serve God in our callings.[b] Nor should we go to law until such time as we have first assayed all other good means of peace and agreement. For a Christian may not love contention, but [he should] account it his wisdom and glory to pass by offenses.[c]

2. That before we seek remedy of our wrongs by the ordinary means we seek first to the Lord[d] and so acknowledge His righteous hand in the wrong that is done us by our enemies as we may be moved to make peace with God and to profit thereby.[e]

3. That the end we aim at in going to law be not the hurt of our enemy but

    i. the glory of God that shines in the execution and manifestation of justice by this His ordinance. And when we thus acknowledge Him the only maintainer of our persons, goods, and credit,[f] and avenger of all wrongs,[g] and dare not revenge ourselves,[g] and

    ii. the necessary defense and maintenance of ourselves and such as God has charged us to have care of,[h] and

    iii. the reformation of the party himself[i] and of others by his example.[j]

4. That we both begin and follow our suits in law without covetousness,[k] using no bitterness[l] and extremity against the person of our adversary.[m] Nor laboring either by bribery or by any other means to corrupt or hinder justice, but so seek our own right as it may appear we are

not void of love and compassion and desire of reconciliation with our adversary.[n]

5. That when we have used these ordinary means that the Lord has given us for the righting of ourselves and find no redress, we must rest with quietness and meekness therein, without fretting or desire to right ourselves by private revenge,[o] knowing assuredly that the Lord has thus ordered the whole matter, either for our correction or for the exercise of our patience and charity.[p] And that He will be revenged of such an enemy and deal far better for us (if we can commit our cause to Him) than either ourselves or any magistrate could have done.[q]

[a] 1 Cor. 6:2
[b] 1 Cor. 6:5–7; Matt. 5:25
[c] Prov. 20:3; 19:11; Phil. 4:5
[d] 2 Chron. 16:12
[e] Deut. 28:29; Lam. 3:39–40
[f] Ps. 3:3
[g] Ps. 94:1–2
[h] 1 Sam. 25:31, 33
[i] Rom. 13:1–10; 1 Tim. 5:8; 2 Cor. 12:1; Eph. 4:2
[j] Eccl. 8:12
[k] Deut. 13:11; 17:13
[l] Heb. 13:5
[m] Eph. 4:31
[n] 2 Chron. 28:9–11; Deut. 24:6; Isa. 58:3; Matt. 18:28
[o] Deut. 24:17; Prov. 17:2
[p] Phil. 4:5; James 5:7–9
[q] Ps. 39:9; 2 Sam. 16:10
[r] Pss. 94:20–23; 37:5–6; 1 Peter 4:19

Question 88: *You have shown that none can be fit to receive this sacrament unless he can find in himself those six graces that are mentioned by you. Tell me now, is this all that is required for our preparation to this sacrament?*

Answer: No, for those that are regenerated and have both faith and repentance and true charity may receive this sacrament unworthily if they be not careful to renew and stir up these graces in themselves at such times as they intend to come unto the Lord's Table.[a]

[a] 1 Cor. 11:30–32

Question 89: *How must we renew our faith when we prepare ourselves to come to the Lord's Table?*

Answer:

1. We must diligently reexamine and try it by the causes and fruits thereof, that we may be more assured it is indeed the lively and justifying faith of God's elect.[a]

2. We must take pains to bring our hearts both to a sight and sense of our infidelity, and of the weakness of our faith,[b] and to a true care and desire to be confirmed in it by this sacrament.[c] Also to an unfeigned resolution to use all good means whereby to strengthen it and to shun the means that may weaken the same.[d]

[a] 2 Cor. 13:5
[b] Mark 9:24
[c] Luke 17:5
[d] Rom. 16:17

Question 90: *How must we renew our repentance when we prepare ourselves to come to the Lord's Table?*

Answer: We must labor to bring our hearts

1. To a sight and sense of our particular sins, especially those which we have fallen into since we last renewed our covenant with God in this sacrament.[a]

2. Unto a true care to cleanse ourselves from them by sincere repentance and [a] desire to obtain both further assurance of the pardon of them and strength against them by receiving of this sacrament.[b]

3. To an unfeigned resolution not to fall into them again but to shun all the shows and occasions of them and to serve God with more conscience and care than heretofore we have done.[c]

[a] Jer. 3:13
[b] 2 Cor. 7:1
[c] Pss. 119:106; 85:8

Question 91: *How must we renew our charity when we prepare ourselves to come unto the Lord's Table?*

Answer: We must endeavor to bring our hearts

1. To a sight and sense of our great want of true love and proneness unto malice and contention.[a]

2. To a true care of reconciliation with all men and willingness to seek it, and [a] desire to receive strength by this sacrament against our uncharitableness, and to be confirmed and increased by it in our unfeigned love to all men, especially to the children of God.[b]

3. To an unfeigned resolution to continue in that unity and love that we make show of at our coming to this sacrament.[c]

[a] James 4:5
[b] Rom. 12:18
[c] Ps. 119:57, 112

Question 92: *You have shown what those graces be that everyone must find in himself that desires to receive this sacrament with comfort, and that it is not sufficient to have them but that a man which has them must also labor to stir them up and renew them in himself at every time when he prepares himself to come to this sacrament. Tell me now, what do you think of them that (though they do find those graces you have mentioned to be in them in some measure) yet do feel them to be so weak and imperfect, and the contrary corruptions so strong,* *that they are much troubled with the sight and sense thereof? May such presume to come to the Lord's Supper with any assurance that they shall receive it worthily?*

Answer: They may [receive worthily] if they can find

1. That those weak graces that are in them are joined with a desire to grow in grace.[a]

2. That the imperfections that they find in themselves be such as they can unfeignedly grieve for and strive against.[b]

3. That the flesh and the corruptions thereof are in them as the old man, dying and decaying continually,[c] and the spirit with the fruits thereof like the new man, always growing and waxing stronger in them.[d]

Yea, such as these, notwithstanding their wants and corruptions, are of all others the fittest to come unto this sacrament.

[a] Mark 9:24
[b] Mark 9:24; Luke 24:17
[c] Eph. 4:22
[d] Eph. 4:22

Question 93: *How may that appear?*

Answer:

1. Because the disciples, whom our Savior Himself admitted to this sacrament in the first institution thereof, were at that time far from perfection and full of infirmities.[a]

2. The Lord's Supper is ordained to confirm our faith and all the fruits of it (which we should have no need of if any grace were perfect in us) and to be the sacrament of our spiritual nourishment, which none can be so fit to receive as they that, out of the sense of their weakness and readiness to faint, do most feel the need they have of it.[b]

3. If none might receive it that feel corruption and want of grace in themselves, then had it been instituted altogether in vain, seeing the best of God's children while they live in the flesh are regenerated but in part.[c] And this does infallibly argue a man to be in the state of grace when he so feels his corruptions and wants that he can grieve for them and strive against them and unfeignedly desire to grow in grace.[d]

[a] Matt. 26:31, 34, 40; Mark 14:40; Luke 22:49–50; Luke 24:11; Mark 16:13–14; Luke 24:45; John 20:9
[b] Rom. 4:11
[c] 1 Cor. 13:9–12; Gal. 5:17
[d] Matt. 5:3, 4, 6; Rom. 7:15–25

Question 94: *You have shown what the points be wherein we must examine ourselves before we come to the Lord's Table. But is this all that we must do in the preparing of our hearts unto this sacrament?*

Answer: No. But we must also (both in secret, before we come unto the public assembly, and when we come there, joining with the congregation) make humble, faithful, and earnest prayer unto God for the pardon of all our sins (specially our coming so oft heretofore to His holy Table with unprepared hearts). [Al]so for His blessing upon that endeavor which we have now used for our preparation, and for His gracious supply of whatsoever has been wanting therein, and for His assistance in this holy action that we are to take in hand.

Question 95: *Is it also necessary to our preparation that we come fasting to this sacrament? Or do they sin and make themselves unworthy receivers of it that do eat or drink anything before they come unto it?*

Answer: No, verily. For though it be not unfit for such as may conveniently do it without hurt or danger to their health to come fasting to this sacrament, yet seeing

1. There is no commandment of God that does enjoin it,[a] and

2. Both at the first institution and long after in the primitive church it was wont to be received after other meat,[b] and

3. The kingdom of God stands not in meat and drink,[c] for neither if we eat have we the more, neither if we eat not have we the less.[d] Therefore, to put holiness in this or to esteem it necessary to the worthy receiving of this sacrament is mere ignorance and superstition.

[a] Deut. 4:1; Isa. 1:12
[b] 1 Cor. 11:22, 34
[c] Rom. 14:17–18
[d] 1 Cor. 8:8

Question 96: *Hitherto you have declared how we must prepare ourselves before we come unto it if we desire to receive this sacrament to our comfort. Tell me now, what is required of us during the time of the administration thereof?*

Answer: [There are] some things that concern the outward behavior and actions of the body, and some things that concern the inward affection and disposition of the heart and mind.

Question 97: *What be those outward things that you say are required of us during the time that this holy action is in hand?*

Answer:

1. As at all other times when we are to join with the congregation in God's service,[a] so especially when we are to receive this sacrament that is appointed of God to be a sign and seal of that most near communion and fellowship that we have with all God's people[b] we must be careful to come all together to the beginning of God's

public worship and to tarry all together till the whole action be finished.[c]

2. As in all other parts of God's public worship, the congregation must join together as one man, and none may either by private devotion, or any other way, withdraw themselves from that which is publicly done.[d] So in this part of God's worship especially, everyone must give diligent attention to that which is done, not only when he himself is ready to receive but [also] during the whole action. [He must] even behold and look upon both the elements themselves and all the sacramental actions that are by Christ's ordinance used in the administration of this sacrament because God has appointed that to be a means to stir up and help our faith in this action.[e]

3. As in all the public worship of God, where the Lord is in a special sort present,[f] much outward reverence and seemly carriage of ourselves is required.[g] So in this whole action, and then especially when [we] ourselves are to receive those holy signs of the body and blood of Christ, we must use such behavior and gesture of our body as may be free from superstition and yet fit to stir up and express that inward faith and thankfulness which is required in the receiving of that which God then does offer unto us.

4. As the works of mercy should always be joined with the works of piety because they do much [to] further the fruit and comfort of all the parts of God's worship,[h] so especially ought everyone, when he has received from God such pledges of His love in this sacrament, according to his ability and in testimony of his thankfulness unto God and love to men, to offer unto God with cheerfulness the sacrifice of alms for the relief of the poor members of Jesus Christ.[i]

[a] Ezek. 46:10
[b] 1 Cor. 10:16–17

^c 1 Cor. 11:17–18, 30–33; Acts 20:7
^d Acts 1:14; 2:1, 46
^e Ex. 24:8
^f Matt. 18:20
^g Lev. 19:30; Ps. 5:7; 1 Cor. 11:10; 14:40
^h Neh. 8:10–12; 1 Cor. 16:1–2
ⁱ Heb. 13:16

Question 98: *As you have shown what is required of us during the time of this action, as touching the outward duty and behavior of our bodies, so tell me now, what should be the meditation and disposition of our hearts at that time?*

Answer:

1. When we see both bread and wine standing upon the Lord's Table, which the minister of Christ has consecrated and put apart to this holy use, then must we with joy of heart call to mind and consider that Jesus Christ was sanctified and put apart to be the only and all-sufficient means of nourishing and preserving us in the state of grace, of strengthening and refreshing our souls in all temptations.[a]

2. When we see this bread broken and this wine poured forth by the minister of Christ, then must we think seriously with grief and indignation of heart of our own sins that pierced Christ and imposed such necessity upon Him to suffer so infinite and unspeakable torments, and withal of the infinite justice of God and His anger against sin that could never have been appeased but by this means.[b]

3. When we see the bread thus broken and the wine thus poured forth to be offered by the minister of Christ unto us, and hear him in Christ's name command us to take, eat, and drink it, then must we with joy and thankfulness of heart meditate of the wonderful love of God toward us,[c] not only in not sparing His own Son, but giving Him

for us, but also in offering Him unto us in His Word and sacrament[28] and commanding us to believe in Him.[d]

4. When we take the bread and the wine at the minister's hand, and do eat and drink the same, then must we stir up our souls by faith to lay hold upon and apply to ourselves all the merits of Christ's passion, fully assuring ourselves that by those unspeakable torments of His own Son the anger of God is fully appeased and His justice satisfied for all our sins,[e] and so joyfully feed thereupon that we may feel our souls not only fully satisfied thereby[f] and strengthened and refreshed against all temptations[g] but also quickened and enabled to walk in all holy obedience unto God.[h]

5. When we behold all the rest of God's people in the same congregation communicating with us in the same elements and sacramental actions without any difference or respect of persons, then must we call to mind and consider how great a corruption it has been in us to despise the church of God, or the least member thereof, and to have been so unkind unto them, so prone to malice them and hard to be reconciled unto them[i] whom God our heavenly Father and Christ our blessed Savior have so dearly loved and done so much for.[j] Yea, we must stir up our hearts to bear a loving and kind affection as to all the people of God, so especially to them that we do communicate withal.

6. When after we have received we give somewhat according to our ability for the relief of the poor, and join with the whole congregation in prayer and singing of psalms, then must we stir up ourselves to do all this with feeling and joy and thankfulness of heart, as unto God that

---

28. *In His Word and sacrament*: this phrase does not appear in the 1609 edition.

loves a cheerful giver[k] and is a Spirit, and will accept of no service but that which is done in spirit and truth.[l] So [we offer] unto Him the sacrifice not of alms[m] only and of the calves of our lips[n] but of our own bodies and souls in thanksgiving for this inestimable benefit of our redemption and for His fatherly care by ordaining this sacrament, to apply it unto us and to confirm our faith in the same.[o]

[a] John 6:27; 10:36; 17:19
[b] Zech. 12:10
[c] John 3:16; Rom. 8:32
[d] 1 John 3:23
[e] Isa. 64:7; Ps. 42:11
[f] John 6:35
[g] Matt. 11:28; John 6:33, 48
[h] John 15:4–5
[i] 1 Cor. 11:21; Matt. 18:10
[j] Rom. 14:15; 1 Cor. 8:11
[k] 2 Cor. 9:7
[l] John 4:23–24
[m] Heb. 13:16
[n] Hos. 14:2
[o] Rom. 12:1

Question 99: *What is the cause why in almost all the parts of that inward disposition that is required of us in this holy action, you make mention of joy? Can we not rightly celebrate this heavenly banquet without inward joy and gladness of heart?*

Answer: No, verily. For as in the celebration of the Passover[a] and of all those solemn feasts that were kept under the law,[b] the people of God were commanded to rejoice and to stir up themselves thereunto by all good means, because no man can indeed be rightly thankful unto God for that blessing wherein he does not rejoice;[c] so in this sacrament especially wherein we are to celebrate with thanksgiving the memory of a benefit that is incomparably greater than ever the church received under the law, this joy and gladness of heart is necessarily required at our hand.[d]

> [a] 2 Chron. 30:21, 26
> [b] Deut. 12:12; 16:15; Neh. 8:10; 1 Sam. 1:7
> [c] Pss. 27:6; 126:2–3; 92:1–4
> [d] 1 Cor. 11:24–25

Question 100: *You have shown how we must prepare ourselves before we come to the Lord's Table and also what disposition of body and mind is required of us at that time when this holy action is in hand. Tell me now, what must we do after we have received, to confirm and increase the comfort and fruit of it in ourselves?*

Answer:

1. So soon as we are come home from the public assembly, we ought in secret to consider and bethink ourselves seriously what we have done and how we have sped, what joy and comfort we have felt in this sacrament, what increase of faith and resolution to lead a holy life we have received thereby. Because we may be sure that no man has received this sacrament worthily, nor fed upon Christ in it (whose flesh is meat indeed and whose blood is drink indeed,[a] and whom none ever touched with a true faith but they received virtue from Him[b]), that has received no refreshing nor strength by it.

2. If we can find no such comfort and fruit that we have received by it, then must we examine diligently whether we may not justly charge ourselves to be the cause thereof because we came not unto it with that preparation of heart as has been described. And if we find the cause wholly in ourselves, then must we presently humble our souls before God in fervent prayer and unfeigned repentance for this our grievous sin, that so judging ourselves for it we may not be judged of the Lord.[c]

3. If, upon diligent examination of our hearts, we can find that this our want of comfort and fruit which we are unfeignedly grieved for arises not thus from our own sin but that we brought with us unto the sacrament (in truth and sincerity, though in much weakness) that preparation of heart that has been described, then have we no just cause to be dismayed in ourselves.[d] But, after that we have humbled our souls before God in prayer for the sanctifying and removing of this His correction which for our trial and other causes best known to Himself He sees good to exercise us by, we may comfort ourselves in this, that such hardness and senselessness of heart which we thus feel and bewail in ourselves may be in them that are in the state of grace.[e] And, our conscience bearing witness with us that we came rightly prepared unto the sacrament, we have undoubtedly received comfort and fruit by it, which we shall also feel hereafter, though we do not for the present.[f]

4. If, upon this examination of our own hearts, we can find that we have sped well at this feast and that the Lord has so welcomed and entertained us at it that we are come from it well refreshed and strengthened in our faith and love and in our resolution to lead a holy life, then must we presently in hearty prayer give thanks unto God for this His unspeakable gift, and crave of Him the continuance and perfecting of His own work that He has wrought in us.[g]

5. The benefit we have received by this sacrament, and comfort in the sense of God's love and favor to us in Christ, as it must provoke us to come oft to this banquet, so must it make us careful to perform our vows we have now made unto God in the presence of all His people[h] by laboring to express the truth of our thankfulness, both in taking heed that we return not again (as the dog to his vomit) unto any of our sins that

we have professed repentance of as also in endeavoring to honor God by a holy obedience to His will, in our whole conversation, all the days of our life.[i]

[a] John 6:55
[b] Mark 5:28–30; 6:56
[c] Lam. 3:39–40; 1 Cor. 11:31
[d] 2 Chron. 30:18–19
[e] Isa. 63:17
[f] Ps. 97:11
[g] 1 Chron. 29:18
[h] Ps. 116:14–18; Eccl. 5:3–4
[i] Ezra 10:11; Ps. 50:23; 106:2–3

Soli Deo gloria